PUSHING THE LIMITS

UNLEASHING THE POTENTIAL OF
STUDENT MINISTRY

PUSHING THE LIMITS

UNLEASHING THE POTENTIAL OF STUDENT MINISTRY

MIKE CALHOUN AND MEL WALKER

NELSON BOOKS
A Division of Thomas Nelson Publishers
Since 1798

www.thomasnelson.com

Published in Nashville, Tennessee, by Thomas Nelson, Inc. www.thomasnelson.com

Nelson Books titles may be purchased in bulk for educational, business, fund-raising, or sales promotional use. For information, please e-mail SpecialMarkets@ThomasNelson.com.

Pushing the Limits

ISBN: 0-8499-0349-1

Printed in the United States of America

1 2 3 4 5 6 — 09 08 07 06

ACKNOWLEDGMENTS

Books aren't just written, they are a process. The process is about words, concepts, and chapters, but primarily it is about people. I am a product of the investment of people in my life. Although I could never acknowledge them all, I want to express my thanks to some of those people who have influenced my life.

Thanks to Ridgecrest Baptist Church for reaching me with the gospel of Christ as a young man. For loving, teaching, and believing in me.

Jack Wyrtzen influenced my life in many ways, and one way was by teaching me to leverage ministries. This book is an outgrowth of that instruction.

Thank you Paul Bubar for teaching me to dream big and to "push the limits."

I am blessed to work with some of God's choice servants in the ministry of Word of Life Fellowship. It is a blessing to be able to work with your best friends.

Mel Walker and all the writers have fanned the flame of my passion for student ministry. They are not just powerful examples of youth leaders, but most of all they are my friends.

My greatest fan club is my family. Thank you to my wife, Betsi, and my children, Misty, Josh, Kim, Caleb, Beth, and Bryan, for believing in me. Your love amazes me.

—Mike Calhoun

This book is a combined effort that reflects literally hundreds of hours of work on the part of so many people. That being said, I can only hope that this brief acknowledgment provides a small token of my expression of thanksgiving to the following people for their contributions to this project.

Mike Calhoun: Thanks so much for your burden to pull off

this project. I appreciate your contacts with writers and your work in editing and arranging the manuscript. Thanks too for your friendship and for your support. I greatly value your big-picture perspective of youth ministry.

The writers of this book: Alex, Ben, Calvin, Cheryl, Dave, Dwight, Eric, Glenn, Lee, Phil, Ric, Steve, Tim, and Tom, thanks for trusting us with your work and for taking a risk to join Mike and me in this idea.

The board of directors at Vision For Youth, Inc.: Tim, Glenn, Don, Jon, Cheryl, Jeff, Abe, Alan, and Matt, thanks for your support of my vision for writing and communicating to youth workers. You'll never know how much I appreciate your involvement in this ministry.

My family: I also want to express my thanks to my wife, Peggy, and my kids—Kristi, Todd, and Travis & Kaci—for your support and encouragement of this book.

—Mel Walker

CONTENTS

INTRODUCTION   ix

LEADING BY TRUTH OR TREND   1
Mike Calhoun

CLUES TO THE CULTURE   11
Glenn Amos

DO YOU KNOW MORE THAN MY NAME?   27
Dwight Peterson

GO WHERE THEY ARE   39
Tim Ahlgrim

MORE THAN COOKIES AND PUNCH   59
Eric Hystad

GOD . . . AND GUITARS   71
Tom Phillips

TEACHING ON PURPOSE WITH A PURPOSE   83
Mel Walker

DID YOU HEAR WHAT I SAID?   99
Lee Vukich & Steve Vandegriff

WHY DO YOU BELIEVE THAT?   111
Alex McFarland

THE "R" WORD THAT CHANGES YOUR MINISTRY   131
Calvin Carr

TEACHING OTHERS TO BE WHAT I ALREADY AM   139
Ric Garland

BUILDING A GREAT STUDENT MINISTRY   149
Ben Brown

CAN A GIRL DO THAT?   163
Dr. Cheryl Fawcett

IT AIN'T NO ONE-MAN SHOW   175
Phil Newberry

WHAT ARE YOU GOING TO BE WHEN YOU GROW UP?   189
Dr. David E. Adams

CONTRIBUTING WRITERS   203

INTRODUCTION

Several years ago, God placed a burden in our hearts for this book. We felt compelled to assemble a group of writers who had ministries tested by time, men and women committed to teaching the truth of the Word and to reaching youth through the local church. Thus began our journey toward this book. The technical term for this book is "anthology" because it is a collection of writings. But once you get into the heart of this work you will discover it is much more, as it represents real life on the front lines of student ministry.

The writers were selected with great care and much prayer. We decided to invite authors whom we personally knew were "push the limits" people. Some have names that are known nationwide, and others may be new to you. Some have other published works, and for some this was their first adventure in writing. For this book, we simply asked them to write about something they were doing, something that may have seemed commonplace to them but that you may find revolutionary. In other words, we asked them to sit down and write about one important principle or practice that unleashes the potential of their student ministries.

Each chapter has been crafted and chiseled out of the granite of experience and conviction. These writers are more than theorists; they are practitioners. They are all students of students, and they have intentionally placed themselves in vulnerable positions in order to influence the church and our culture. Our writers come from a variety of backgrounds and experiences, but they all share the same passion for student ministry. Uniquely, they are all committed to student ministry in the local church while functioning in a variety of venues. There is a solidarity of ministry philosophy here that is implemented through different methodologies.

Each writer has earned a place in this book by his or her track record—not the size of the ministry. They represent ministries that have quantifiable benchmarks for coaching students and student leaders to maturity in Christ. All were given a topic based on an evaluation of their ministry and were invited to write on a subject representing an obvious strength. What they have written is a journal chronicling their actual experiences rather than what they have envisioned. It is one thing to point the way to great student ministry, but it is powerful when you can lead others by personal example.

In terms of the ministries with which they are associated, some represent large churches with coffee shops inside them, others have faithfully performed their calling in churches that might fit inside your local coffee shop. Their lives are not about bricks and mortar but about students growing in faith. Most of the writers travel nationally and internationally to speak to students and leaders, while some have focused their lives on a particular ZIP code. In these pages, you will find an array of youth pastors who have walked in your shoes and who can truly understand the struggles you are facing. And because training and development of future youth workers and pastors is critical, we also have asked some of America's top Christian educators to share from their experiences.

Youth ministry consultants play a strategic role in local church student ministries today. Some of our writers have given their lives to coming alongside youth pastors and leaders to offer encouragement and instruction through their parachurch youth ministry organization. This combined perspective of writers created an unlimited potential resource for student ministry that changes lives.

Student ministry has always pushed the limits. From its roots in the early youth rallies and prayer meetings to the modern youth workers' conventions, the trail of student ministry has been blazed by visionary risk-takers who saw an incredible need and were willing, by the grace of God, to do something about it. Our prayer is that this book would follow that pursuit as well. It is in that sense that we want to encourage readers to unleash the amazing potential of student ministry.

As you read this book, our prayer is that you will become uncomfortable. There is a difference between being content and being satisfied. We are admonished by Scripture to be content, but we think becoming satisfied with ministry is a tool of the devil. We want you to determine to push the limits of ministry, to think outside the lines. We hope this book will challenge you in such a way that neither you nor your students will ever be the same. Go ahead, push the limits and unleash the potential of your student ministry!

Mike and Mel

PUSHING THE LIMITS

UNLEASHING THE POTENTIAL OF
STUDENT MINISTRY

LEADING BY TRUTH OR TREND

Mike Calhoun

David could not believe his ears! Sarah was one of his sharpest teens, not one of the fringe kids who resisted involvement. For just a moment he felt numb, and then he mumbled something to her like, "Well, I guess that will be OK, if you really don't want to." As he drove home from the church, her words kept rolling around in his mind. Sarah had looked him right in the eyes and said, "David, I love God, but I don't have time for daily devotions or memorizing Scripture. I am just too busy, and I have to prioritize my life. I am sure God understands; I just wanted you to know."

What Sarah said had stunned him initially, and as he drove home, he questioned his reply to her comment. What should he have said to her? Is it really no big deal if she does not spend time with the Lord in His Word each day? Did she have a busy schedule or just misplaced priorities? Are there really "irreducible minimums" for the Christian life and, if so, where are they found?

David was experiencing the same thing that many other youth leaders and youth pastors have confronted in their youth groups. Can you relate to David and his feelings of confusion? Can you feel his pain? He wondered what he should have said and how he should have handled the situation.

David is a real person, and this incident really occurred. Just like hundreds of other youth pastors around the nation, David is just one of those who questions where to go for definitive answers and effective guidance. Perhaps he, like so many others, will discover the answer in a ministry founded on biblical principles. Having a principle-centered ministry will never stop these types of dialogues, but it will give you definition for articulating direction and truth. It will definitely prevent an anemic response like, "Well, I guess that will be OK, if you really don't want to."

Years ago, I searched the Scriptures for my own personal biblical foundation. I wanted to establish the "irreducible minimums" for my ministry—the nonnegotiables, if you please. Then one day I was reading Colossians 1:9–14. It was as if they leapt off the page at me. Right there in those few verses was my ministry plumb line. Obviously, the foundation for all of our ministries is found in the principles of Scriptures. God is the Source of all absolute truth. A. W. Tozer said, "He is the plumb line by which all actions and thoughts will be judged." The Word of God becomes not only our foundation, but also our plumb line by which we measure everything we do in ministry.

> For this reason we also, since the day we heard it, do not cease to pray for you, and to ask that you may be filled with the knowledge of His will in all wisdom and spiritual understanding; that you may walk worthy of the Lord, fully pleasing Him, being fruitful in every good work and increasing in the knowledge of God; strengthened with all might, according to His glorious power, for all patience and longsuffering with joy; giving thanks to the Father who has qualified us to be partakers of the inheritance of the saints in the light. He has delivered us from the power of darkness and conveyed us into the kingdom of the Son of His love, in whom we have redemption through His blood, the forgiveness of sins.
>
> Colossians 1:9–14

Some commentators have called this Paul's target prayer for the Colossians. You can sense his deep burden for these believers to move from spiritual apathy to a healthy relationship with Christ. Paul's sincere prayer for the Colossians provided the mandates upon which to build my own life and ministry.

As you read Colossians 1:9–14, what are some of Paul's special concerns for the Colossians? Perhaps your answer would be:

- Maturity
- Knowledge of God
- Fruitfulness
- Prayer
- Spiritual wisdom
- Knowledge of His will

FOUNDATIONAL MINISTRY PRINCIPLES

In this section of Scripture, Paul has given us a biblical outline of some foundational ministry principles. He has given some "irreducible minimums" to follow as we create our biblical philosophy. Paul's prayer describes a specific pattern of growth for the believers. What Paul defines is an incredible outline for ministry! These are the things we want to accomplish—the goals we want to attain in the lives of young people—regardless of what else we produce. I have illustrated it as a target to demonstrate the flow.

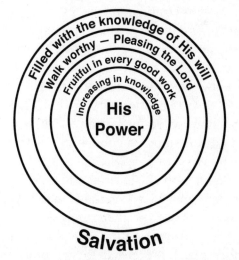

Let's begin with verse fourteen, as it is foundational to the passage. Paul addresses this letter to people who are already saved: "in whom we have redemption through His blood, the forgiveness of sins." This is written to the Colossian believers in the church of Colosse. Paul is praying specifically for certain things to happen in their lives.

SALVATION

Salvation must come before spiritual growth and sanctification. The obvious primary concern for a young person's life must be salvation. This is the first irreducible minimum of ministry. Our passion should be to see youth turned "from darkness to light, and from the power of Satan to God" (Acts 26:18).

FILLED WITH THE KNOWLEDGE OF HIS WILL

Once we know they have new life in Christ, our desire should be for them to grow spiritually. The second irreducible minimum is found in verse nine: "that you may be filled with the knowledge of His will." Without a doubt the number one question I am asked by young people as well as adults is, "How do I know the will of God for my life?" Every serious believer wants to know how to determine God's will.

I will never forget praying as a freshman in college about a summer mission's ministry. I had been praying and searching the Scripture, but I was struggling with how to make the right decision. I went to one of the deacons in my church and asked, "How do I know God's will for my life?" His answer was, "You know the will of God by the Word of God." This is a true statement, but without some further direction, it was just a Christian cliché to me. It sounded good, but how to appropriate it in my own life was a bit of a puzzle.

So that night, with all sincerity and an earnest heart, I took out my Bible and opened it. I reasoned that if "you know the will of God by the Word of God" then surely God would direct me to a passage of Scripture giving me clear direction concerning the choices before me. I proceeded to randomly open the Bible, dropping my finger onto the page, and then began to read what I was convinced would be the answer to my search for His will.

Thinking back on this now, it is a bit humorous—but it was

not funny at the time. It was confusing. I began to read and discovered I was right in the middle of a genealogy. I knew it was not God's will for me to "beget" thirty-two kids that summer. Then I thought to myself, "I am a New Testament believer, so I probably will discover my answer there." I flipped over a few pages and opened my Bible to the New Testament. Once again I dropped my finger to the page in desperate search for direction. This is the truth: I did not make this up. I read the verse directly under my finger and this is what it said, "And he went out and hanged himself." I realized I was not doing well with this method of discovering God's will. At this point there seemed to be two options: I can have thirty-two kids or go out and hang myself. Neither was appealing or relevant to my situation.

You and I do discover the will of God by the Word of God . . . that is true. The Spirit of God may direct us to some particular passage, but it is not by the ole "blind spiritual finger" approach that God reveals His will. As we study the Word of God, we learn its principles and, as the truths become a part of our lives, it is wonderful to see what happens. The Spirit of God uses the Word of God to give us direction. This concept also begs the question, "How much of the will of God do we really want to know?" If the answer is "just a little," then we spend little time in the Bible. But if our desire is to truly know His will, then we will give priority to our time with the Scriptures.

Being "filled with the knowledge of His will" does not come by infrequent association with the Bible or by casually skimming Scripture. Searching and studying the Scriptures, and memorizing and meditating on the Word, provide ammunition for the Spirit of God to use in our lives each day. Somehow we've gotten to the place where we think God's will is ethereal or mysterious, something we can't really grab a hold of or understand. The will of God is not mysterious or impossible to discover. If that were true then why would Paul pray for them to be filled with God's will?

Another area that clouds our understanding of the will of God is praying for things out of ignorance. You may ask, "Are there things we do not need to pray about?" The answer is "Yes!" I am personally convinced that many of the things we pray about have already been revealed to us in the Scriptures; it is just that we are biblically ignorant. Matthew 22:29 tells us, "You are mistaken [you go the wrong way], not knowing the Scriptures nor the power of God." If we knew more of the Word of God, then we would know more of the will of God.

After speaking at a youth activity, I was approached by a young lady who asked, "Would you pray for me?"

"What about?"

She replied, "Well, I'm dating this unsaved guy, and I want you to pray for me as I determine whether God wants me to marry him or not."

I know that I surprised her when I answered, "No. I'm sorry, but I will not pray for you about that."

She raised her voice and said, "You are a preacher, and you are supposed to pray for people!"

"That's right," I told her, "and I will pray for you. But I cannot pray for you concerning that request." She was very indignant even when I explained my response. "I don't need to pray about something that God has already addressed clearly in His Word."

God has revealed much of His will for believers in His Word. We do not need to seek direction through prayer for questions that have already been answered. What we need to do is to get into the Word of God and let the Word of God get into us. John 15:7 says, "If you abide in Me, and My words abide in you, you will ask what you desire, and it shall be done for you." My deacon was correct when he said, "You know the will of God by the Word of God." He had pointed me in the right direction, yet he failed to mention the landmarks for discovering God's will through His Word.

WALK WORTHY—PLEASING THE LORD

Paul continues his prayer to the Colossians with the words, "That you might walk worthy of the Lord unto all pleasing." Here is the third irreducible minimum. I suggest we adopt it in our ministries. Not only must we "walk worthy," pleasing the Lord, but also it is imperative that we help others to do likewise. In particular, we are talking about helping students know how to please the Lord. This is the dilemma we face when working with those who have a casual acquaintance with God. I have never met most of you who are reading this book. I know nothing about you and your personal likes or dislikes. If I met you tomorrow and wanted to do something to please you, it would be difficult because I do not know what brings a smile to your face. Or perhaps you would want to do something nice that would please me. So the next time you see me, you may give me a roast beef sandwich covered in mayonnaise. No matter how nice you are trying to be, you will only do this because you don't know me. Those who know me know I cannot stand mayonnaise. I get dry heaves just looking at a jar containing the substance. There is no way for you to know this if you do not know me.

On the other hand, I have some very close friends. We have spent a great deal of time together in a variety of situations. We have laughed, cried, and prayed together. It would not be difficult for me to do something for them, nor for them to do something for me that would bring great joy to each of our lives. What is the difference in the two scenarios? The difference is in the relationship. I know what pleases my close friends but not those with whom I only have a casual acquaintance.

The only way we can walk worthy of the Lord and please Him is if we truly know Him. In John 8:29, Jesus says, "For I always do those things that please Him." The Lord Jesus Christ always did the things that pleased His Heavenly Father. That's what we ought to do. But the only way we can please our Heavenly Father is if we have an intimate relationship with Him. As we read the Word of God, do you know what we find? On a daily basis we find the things that please and displease Him. As we read the Word of God, we discover the mind of Christ, which helps us to know what is important. So you and I need to walk worthy, pleasing the Lord and helping our young people to do the same.

FRUITFUL IN EVERY GOOD WORK

Paul's irreducible minimum for the Colossians, and the fourth one I want to mention, comes in verse ten as he moves to the aspect of fruit-bearing in the Christian life. "Being fruitful in every good work" means communicating the truth of the Word of God to a lost generation. We want them to know Jesus Christ personally. Very simply, Paul is reminding us that everywhere we go—in everything we do—we ought to take every opportunity as an occasion to share the good news of the gospel.

Paul says, "in every good work," so this is not relative to sharing the gospel. Paul is challenging us to live for Christ so that our whole lives are testimonies of His grace. People who live like this are refreshing. Every area of their lives are affected by what they believe. There is no dichotomy between what they believe and how they live. When this is true in a person's life, then pleasing the Lord and fruit bearing are natural responses. You do not have to hang a sign on an apple tree that says, "By the way, you're supposed to bear fruit." It's a natural outgrowth of something that's taking place inside.

INCREASING IN THE KNOWLEDGE OF GOD

Paul's fifth irreducible minimum may strike you as strange coming at this point in the passage. Here he challenges the believers with the phrase, "increasing in the knowledge of God." We begin by "being filled with the knowledge of His will," by "fully pleasing Him" by walking worthy, and by "being fruitful in every good work." This is where most believers stop. We say, "OK, that's it! This is the ultimate. I am bearing fruit so what else is there to the Christian life?" Bearing fruit is a fundamental part of our relationship with Christ, but it is not the end of the growth process.

Right in the middle of this challenge to active faith, Paul reminds us of a vital priority of the Christian life. While we are discovering God's will, walking worthy, and being fruitful, we need to keep increasing in the knowledge of God—knowing our Lord more and more intimately. That may not sound significant, but it is essential. It is easy to get caught up in ministry and activities and forget to cultivate our relationship with Christ. If we do not feed on His Word regularly and practice His presence faithfully, we will become anemic and "weary in well doing."

What keeps us growing? What keeps us effective and efficient in ministry? What keeps our impact level high? It happens when we continue to increase in the knowledge of God. The challenge before us is to create a desire within the youth to grow in Christ. We need tools and methods to stimulate them while serving as vehicles for personal growth. Areas such as daily devotions, Bible study, Scripture memorization, and Christian reading all need to be engrafted into each life if any of us are to increase in the knowledge of God. Any tools we can provide to aid them in their intake of the Scriptures will act as catalysts for learning more about God. Our goal is to get them into the Word so it can get into them. Isaiah 55:10–11 reminds us that the Word of God will not return void, so exposure to the Word is critical.

STRENGTHENED WITH HIS MIGHT

All of this may sound a bit overwhelming and maybe even impossible. So how do we accomplish this in our lives and the lives of our youth? The key according to Paul is God's power. He gives us the sixth and final irreducible minimum in verse eleven when he says, "Strengthened with all might, according to his glorious power." We're strengthened or enabled with His power. The issue we often face in relation to spiritual growth is trying to do it in our own power. We have our rituals, routines, and checklists; but none of those things necessarily energizes us spiritually. Each may have its place in helping us become more accountable, but operating by our own power becomes taxing and wearisome. It is easy to depend upon ourselves—but once we do that, we're in trouble. Paul reminds us in 2 Corinthians 3:5 that "our sufficiency is from God."

Paul's target prayer for the Colossian church not only gives direction for a biblical approach to ministry, but also serves as a plumb line. With this as a guide, we now can evaluate every-thing we do in ministry based upon a scriptural grid. We estab-lish our philosophy of ministry on this foundation.

This passage of Scripture has served as my personal ministry foundation, and I use it to illustrate how to formulate a biblically based ministry. A biblical framework for ministry permeates the Word of God. You may discover it in one passage as I did or in multiple verses in various books of the Bible. This is just one protocol for ministry and is the one God has used in my life.

There are a million great ideas, strategies, programs, and plans out there for youth ministry. So how do we distinguish between a good idea that will contribute to our overall purpose and just another thing to do? Having a biblical basis for min-istry such as the one found in Colossians 1 gives us a plumb line by which to judge.

For example, we may ask ourselves the following questions: Does this idea or program help my youth to be filled with the knowledge of His will? Will it assist them in walking worthy and pleasing the Lord? Will it contribute to their fruitfulness? Will it stimulate them to continue increasing in the knowledge of God? Will it point them to His power or to self-reliance?

Every new idea or program should be held up to the blue-print of biblical mandates. If they fit on the biblical foundation, then they may be adopted and implemented. If they do not, then it becomes easier to discard them without second-guess-ing yourself. If you have determined the irreducible minimums based on biblical mandate, then you can be confident in your dealings with young people who are living "program" lives. When they tell you they do not like Scripture memory or have no time for daily devotions, then your instruction to them can come from biblical principles, not worldly pressures.

So have you taken the time to discover your biblical plumb line? Have you defined the irreducible minimums for your youth ministry? Doing this is one more step in experiencing a ministry founded on truth and not trend. It is both freeing and rewarding to approach life from a biblical framework.

CLUES TO THE CULTURE

Glenn Amos

As I write this chapter, the newspaper headlines read, "School gunman kills 9!" The article continues, "A Minnesota high school student killed nine people and wounded several others Monday in the worst school-shooting case since the Columbine massacre in Colorado in 1999."[1]

The timing of this incident is ironic. To many adults, this shooting only adds to the perception that today's youth are as bad as they've ever been, maybe worse. However, the emphasis of this chapter is that today's teenagers are unlike previous generations and "are beginning to manifest a wide array of positive social habits that older Americans no longer associate with youth, including a new focus on teamwork, achievement, modesty, and good conduct.[2]

I'm a baby boomer. That means I was a teenager in the 1960s and watched the church try to figure out how to respond to the Beatles, Woodstock, hippies, "free love," the drug culture, and bell-bottom pants. Most local church youth ministries relied on Sunday night "Youth Group" meetings and the Saturday night "Youth Rallies" to immunize us against all that was happening in our world. Youth rallies were famous for high-energy preachers who screamed at us about sex, drugs, and rock 'n roll and left us feeling as if we were guilty of all three to the greatest extent possible!

Looking back on those days, it is obvious that the church was reacting to the symptoms of a youth culture that it had not taken the time to understand. There was little effort expended to discern what was in the heart of a generation that was so outwardly different from previous generations. Neither was there much of an attempt to identify and articulate a solution based on solid biblical principles.

As a result, I am convinced that the church lost, or chased away, a significant part of my generation. First as teenagers and then as college students, boomers left the church because, to them, it was uninterested, irrelevant, and out of touch. This was a generation whose attitudes were shaped by some of the most turbulent and unnerving events in the history of our nation: the Cuban missile crisis, the assassinations of President John F. Kennedy and Martin Luther King, the Vietnam War and its multi-faceted protests, inner-city race riots, the death of four college students killed by National Guardsmen at Kent State University, and Watergate. As students "turned on and tuned out" in an attempt to find meaning in life, the church missed a huge opportunity to impact my generation with the message of abundant life through a personal relationship with Jesus Christ. The church was guilty of the same thing as Samuel when God sent him to anoint the next king of Israel (cf. 1 Samuel 16)— looking on the "outward appearance" rather than the heart!

I believe the church is again facing a great opportunity to significantly influence a generation of students. However, it is imperative that we take the time to look beyond the "outward appearance," even though it may be far more positive than that of the boomers, and get to the heart of the Millennial Generation.

WHO ARE THEY?

This generation has been labeled Generation Y, as if picking up right where Generation X left off. This appears to be the name used most often by the media. The names Baby Boomlet or Echo Boomers are used to emphasize the obvious connection to their parents, the Baby Boomers. Thom Rainer refers to them as "The Bridgers" because they "will bridge two centuries and two millennia," and it is a name that suggests "hope and promise" as a generation that just might provide a "bridge be-tween the secular and the sacred.[3] Another name worth noting has been coined by George Barna. He uses the name "Mosaics" as a "multifaceted term" that best describes their "eclectic lifestyles . . . nonlinear style of thinking . . . racially integrated relationships . . . core values formation . . . informational con-nection to the Internet . . . and central spiritual tenets."[4]

However, in 1997, ABC's Peter Jennings conducted a poll in order to determine the preferred name for this generation. The Millennial Generation or Millennials came out on top.[5] The significance of this name is that it has no connection to the previous generations. Neil Howe and William Strauss con-ducted many interviews with Millennials and shared this re-sponse from Lesley Milner, age eighteen, as typical of this generation:

> Instead of giving us our own name, someone—proba-bly someone who doesn't know much about us—just said, "Hmm, well, this is Generation X, so why don't we call the next one Generation Y?" Or, "Well, they're the children of boomers, so we can just call them Echo Boom." Neither of these two names says anything unique about our generation. They say who we follow, but nothing at all about who we are.[6]

Due to its widespread use, it would appear that the name "Mil-lennials" has become the name of choice.

So who are the Millennials? They aren't just the children of boomers or a continuation of Gen X. They already have an identity and a reputation of their own: "Millennial attitudes and behaviors represent a sharp break from Generation X, and are running exactly counter to trends launched by the boomers. Across the board, Millennial kids are challenging a long list of common assumptions about what 'postmodern' young people are supposed to become."[7] Much of the research and writing on this generation of students indicates that Millennials believe it is their responsibility to change the world! Here's what else we know about them: they were born between 1982 and 2002[8] and for the most part, are children of baby boomers. That makes the first high school graduating class of the Millennial Generation the Class of 2000. The national birth rate for the Millennials reached its highest point in 1990 at 4.2 million, and the number of high school seniors is expected to peak in 2009. They are over 80 million strong, and demographers predict they will become the largest generation in history topping out at over 100 million.[9] For those working in youth ministry, the sheer size of this generation means that we have our work cut out for us for many years to come!

WHAT ARE THEY LIKE?

The Millennials have been analyzed, characterized, categorized, and compartmentalized to the degree that a CBS News article reported, "they are already one of the most studied generations in history—by sociologists, demographers, and marketing consultants."[10] It is not my intent to identify new attitudes, beliefs, or values of the Millennials, but rather to highlight some of the research and writing that has already been done and to emphasize some of the findings that I believe deserve the most attention from those involved in local church youth ministry.

Howe and Strauss have organized their research data and study of Millennial trends into seven core traits that they say will define this generation over the next few years. "Evidence will mount that Millennials are: special . . . sheltered . . . confident . . . team-oriented . . . conventional . . . pressured . . . and achieving."[11] Daniel Egeler says their behavior and attitudes are "significantly different" from those of the two previous generations, and that, "This attitude shift is particularly noticeable in terms of this generation's (1) optimism, (2) achievement orientation, (3) desire for rules and boundaries, (4) acceptance of authority with a corresponding support of traditional values, and (5) desire to commit to a cause."[12] Claire Raines finds them to be sociable, optimistic, talented, well-educated, collaborative, open-minded, achievement-oriented, confident, hopeful, civic-minded, and inclusive.[13]

Other observations indicate that this generation is also characterized by technological and media sophistication, positive expectations, morality, structured environments, street smarts, parental involvement, heroic spirits, diversity, high self-esteem, friendships, happiness, consumerism, insatiable desires for leisure and entertainment, desires for spiritual meaning and purpose.

WHAT ARE WE GOING TO DO WITH THEM?

One of the characteristics that jumps out of the research is the change in parents' involvement in the lives of their Millennial teens. I accepted the call to my first youth pastorate in the summer of 1978 and immediately began to look for books to read and conferences to attend so that I could learn as much as possible about youth ministry. I discovered that there wasn't much of either at the time. However, as youth ministry began to "come of age" in the 1980s, regional and national conferences for youth workers began to spring up all across the country, inspired by Youth Specialties' National Youth Workers Convention. As those of us in youth ministry soaked up all we could about how to work with teenagers, it became all too obvious that we also needed to learn how to work with their parents.

It wasn't too long before one of the regular topics of discussion among youth workers was, "How can we involve parents in youth ministry?" During the 1980s, Christian schools were booming, local church youth ministries were exploding, and the "generation gap" between parents and teens was widening. Many parents became frustrated with their kids and, intentionally or unintentionally, abdicated their responsibility for the spiritual growth of their teens to the Christian school and/or youth ministry. To make matters worse, many youth pastors were all too willing to accept it!

Our hearts were in the right place, but we weren't asking the right question. We should have been asking, "How can we *help parents* fulfill their God-given responsibility for the spiritual growth and development of their kids?" It has never been the responsibility of the local church to do for students what God intended their parents to do for them. I am convinced that the so-called "adversarial relationship" that stereotypically exists between many parents and youth pastors is a direct result of a misplaced or wrongfully accepted responsibility, a kind of "role reversal" if you will.

It is time for this generation of youth pastors to get beyond the "adversarial relationship," learn from the mistakes of the past, and take advantage of the opportunity that exists to work with Millennial parents. Colleges and universities all across our country are observing that parents are more involved in the lives of their students from the start of the application process to their arrival on campus than before. So much so that Wake Forest University admissions personnel nicknamed them "helicopter parents" . . . because they're "always hovering"[14] Research now shows that the generation gap between parents and teens is smaller than at any other time in the history of polling.[15]

Furthermore, "in a 1998 teen survey, 80 percent reported having had 'really important talks' with their parents, and 94 percent mostly or totally agreed that, 'I can always trust my parents to be there when I need them.' (Back in 1974, more than 40 percent of boomers flatly declared they'd 'be better off not living with their parents.')"[16] George Barna's research found that the greatest influence on the beliefs and practices of teenagers were parents: "Half said that their parents have the greatest influence on their spiritual development, identified three times as often as the next most prolific source of faith influence."[17] And finally, the recently released National Survey of Youth and Religion stated, "For better or worse, most parents in fact still do profoundly influence their adolescents—often more than do their peers . . . the most important social influence in shaping young people's religious lives is the religious life modeled and taught to them by their parents."[18]

Because parents *are* very involved in the lives of their teens, parents *are* the greatest influences in the spiritual development of their teens, and teens *are* closer to their parents than previous generations, youth workers have a huge window of opportunity to help parents disciple their teens in ways that could significantly impact the church and a lost world for eternity! This generation of students wants to be led. They are looking for spiritual authenticity in their parents and in the church. We must help parents understand that they can make a difference in the lives of their teens and then work with them to make sure it happens!

Without getting into the specifics of what this parent-youth ministry alliance should look like in your church, let me conclude with this principle that will work in all churches: "The best way to get most youth more involved in and serious about their faith communities is to get their parents more involved in and serious about their faith communities."[19] Enough said. We must "strike while the iron is hot!"

As youth workers, we must recognize that many of our students do not have parents involved in their lives. Many come from broken homes, single-parent homes, or no home. This is another reason why we are such vital parts of students' lives. We may become surrogate parents, and the church may be the only safe home they know.

Another window of opportunity lies in taking advantage of this generation's strong bent towards team orientation, collaboration, and relationships. Barna says, "There are two key elements that teenagers feel must be incorporated into their experience. The first of those is relationships. . . . Take away relationships and you steal the heart of their world."[20] This is the generation that grew up playing team sports from the time they could walk. Remember the "soccer mom" phenomenon? School uniforms became an accepted practice, and entire schools were designed and built to foster group learning. "If you go into a public school today, teamwork is stressed every-where. Team teaching, team grading, collaborative sports, com-munity service, service learning, student juries. I mean, the list goes on and on."[21]

I began graduate school in 1986 and soon immersed myself in my first research project. Since I had the option of choosing a topic that was relevant to my ministry, I chose to study "peer pressure." You couldn't do youth ministry in those days without hearing that peer pressure was to blame for much of what was wrong in local church youth groups. Peer pressure was consid-ered a negative thing and the motivator of clique formation. From a youth ministry perspective, *cliques* were "small groups of friends formed around common interests that became mu-tually exclusive of other cliques and unattached individuals in the youth group." Membership in a clique was a much sought-after position and was a more powerful influence in the life of a teenager than that of their parents. It was this influence of a group of teens on each other within their own clique, usually in a negative direction, that was called "peer pressure."

We had cleverly designed strategies called "clique busters" to break these cliques and get them to intermingle or fellow-ship with others in the youth group. Ultimately, the desired outcome of these strategies was the dream of all youth pastors . . . unity in the youth group! Looking back on this era of youth ministry and its peer pressure problems, I believe we would have experienced more success and unity by finding a solution designed to keep the cliques together rather than tearing them apart. After all, cliques were nothing more than groups of friends that liked being together because of common interests and desires.

That's what is so encouraging about this generation; they want to be together because they value friendships. In fact, for the first time in years, "peer pressure" is again being discussed in the context of understanding and working with the Millen-nial generation: "This Millennial cliquishness has made peer pressure a much more important teen issue than before, and they see more positive potential in it than adults normally do."[22] Leslie Goldgehn, in her article, "Generation Who, What, Y? What You Need to Know About Generation Y," writes, "Though individuality is significant and should not be under-estimated, 'fitting in' is of equal importance to them. They feel very strongly about living up to the expectations of their peers and their communities."[23]

You see, youth pastors do have another chance to harness the power of cliques, peer pressure, and friendships in order to influence their youth groups, churches, and communities for Christ! I believe Paul wrote about "cliquishness" in a very posi-tive way when he called it the church, "the body of Christ" (see Rom. 12:5). We need to challenge our students with this bibli-cal illustration of teamwork and collaboration. It perfectly combines the emphasis on the individuality and unique gifted-ness of each member of the body with an unmistakable focus on the body as a whole and its need to work together for the good of the body and the glory of God.

As youth workers, our task is clear: we must help them to understand and to live up to God's expectations, taking advan-tage of their desire to please their peers, communities (church, youth group, cliques, etc.), and ultimately their God. The often used and sometimes worn-out acrostic for TEAM, "Together Everyone Achieves More," really does capture the emphasis of this section and will reverberate in the hearts of this genera-tion.

The Millennials are also a generation that is highly confi-dent, optimistic, and achievement oriented. This is the genera-tion that stopped the slide in average SAT scores and recorded the highest average national SAT score sine 1974.[24] Research in-dicates that this is also a generation that will "go beyond just desiring to commit to a cause; they are much more prone to voluntarily contribute their time toward what they feel are wor-thy endeavors."[25] More than the two previous generations, this generation is poised to make a difference. All the indicators are pointing in the same direction; Millennials are ready to step up to the plate and become the next generation of heroes and heroines. As a result of their research, Howe and Strauss believe they will be like their grandparents, the World War II generation, "You can understand how today's kids are on track to become a powerhouse generation . . . perhaps destined to dominate the twenty-first century like today's fading G.I. Generation dominated the twentieth. Indeed, Millennials have a solid chance to become America's next great generation."[26]

So what does this mean for local church youth ministry? It means the students that you work with are ready to be challenged to invest their lives in serving God. It is true that they are focused on higher education and pursuing a career that will provide for their every desire. But if we will strategically build "Great Commission" ministry and passion into their lives for the four to six years we have them under our youth ministry care, maybe they will consider the needs of God's harvest field. Challenge them with the heroes and heroines of the faith: Enoch, Noah, Abraham, Joseph, Moses, Joshua, Rahab, Deborah, Gideon, Ruth, Hannah, Esther, Mary, and the list goes on.

Take advantage of the wide array of ministry opportunities that are on your doorstep: rescue missions, prison ministry, open-air evangelism, random acts of kindness, mission trips, camp counseling, See You at the Pole, not to mention the multitude of opportunities in your own local church. Barna's research showed that "nine out of ten teenagers (89 percent) contend that it is still feasible to think that one human being can make a difference in the world."[27] Challenge them, train them, encourage them, push them, stretch them, but most of all, don't sell them short. If you do, they'll do great things anyway, it just won't matter for eternity!

The most exciting and yet potentially the most heartbreaking characteristic of the Millennial Generation is their interest in spirituality. George Barna's study led him to this conclusion, "Most teens are highly interested in spirituality, but comparatively few are engaged in the pursuit of spiritual depth . . . by their own admission they are only minimally committed to their alleged faith of choice (i.e., Christianity) and to the spiritual practices that will supposedly lead them to spiritual maturity."[28] I said earlier in this chapter that we as youth workers have our work cut out for us. The issue of authentic spiritual commitment is where the "rubber meets the road." An opportunity to influence the spiritual growth, development, and effectiveness of this generation and their parents is in the hands of the local church and its youth ministry team. Walt Mueller of The Center for Parent/Youth Understanding describes the opportunity this way, "Today, kids show up and assume the encouraging posture of engaged skepticism. They want to talk about spiritual things. They are even excited to talk about the Christian faith and biblical truth. The challenge, however, is that they are skeptical about its validity."[29]

Students will question the validity of the Christian faith if they don't understand it or if they don't see those promoting it living as if they believe it. It's not rocket science! As parents, pastors, youth workers, church members, and Christ-followers, we should know what we believe, and those beliefs should affect our lives 24–7. I am convinced that many teens and adults who regularly attend our churches don't know what they believe. I have watched the flow of youth ministry over the last two decades become more entertainment-oriented and less committed to the regular and consistent teaching of the Bible. In many youth ministry settings, relevance in teaching or preaching has been defined as humorous stories, illustrations, and anecdotes with a verse thrown in at the end. Publishers of youth curricula have been watering down their materials for years. Their emphasis has been mainly "learning activities," to the detriment of solid biblical exposition. Their rationale would be that most students can't handle deep teaching, and that's not what the churches want.

In the National Study of Youth and Religion, authors Christian Smith and Melinda Lundquist Denton share some very sobering statistics for local church youth ministry as it relates to students not being able to articulate what they believe. "If there is indeed a significant number of American teens who are serious and lucid about their religious faith, there is also a much larger number who are remarkably inarticulate and befuddled about religion . . . one finds little evidence that the agents of religious socialization in this country are being highly effective and successful with the majority of their young people."[30] Before you convince yourself that *your* students *are* "lucid" about their faith, think about these findings:

> 33 percent of conservative Protestant youth maybe or definitely believe in reincarnation, 33 percent in astrology, 31 percent in communicating with the dead, and 21 percent in psychics and fortune-tellers. For a tradition that has so strongly emphasized the infallibility or inerrancy of the Bible, the exclusive claims of conservative Christianity, and the need for a personal commitment of one's life to God, some of these numbers are astounding. Even the conservative Protestants evidence a great deal of slippage in the effectiveness of the Christian education of their youth.[31]

It is crucial that our students know what they believe. It is crucial that we teach them the Word of God. And it is crucial that we teach it in a dynamic and relevant fashion that is obvious in our lives and will be obvious in theirs as well. Thom Rainer's challenge is most appropriate: "Now is not the time to dumb down our teachings and expectations. More than ever, our Sunday Schools need to increase expectations and challenge the Bridgers (Millennials) with the cost of discipleship clearly taught in Scripture . . . our churches must teach them the counsel of God in the Bible."[32] It is time to get back to building our churches and youth ministries on the solid teaching and preaching of the Word of God. I don't know how to say it any better than that!

I have described the tip of the iceberg when it comes to understanding the heart of the Millennial Generation. Much research and writing already exists. Smith and Denton's book has a wealth of information that serious youth pastors must read, digest, and implement in their own ministries. Theologically speaking, the Millennium (the literal one-thousand-year reign of Christ on the earth) has not arrived. This generation, no matter how different and positive they may be, still needs a personal relationship with God through faith alone in Jesus Christ. They desperately need to experience the abundant life that He has promised. Scriptures tell us that things in the last days will get worse and worse. However, if the door of opportunity to influence a generation is open just a hair wider than it has ever been before, we better figure out how to walk through it.

"The millennial generation may be the single greatest challenge facing the church of Jesus Christ today. But they may also be the single greatest opportunity facing the church today."[33]

NOTES

1. "School gunman kills 9," *USA Today*, March 23, 2005.
2. Neil Howe and William Strauss, *Millennials Rising: The Next Great Generation* (New York: Random House, 2000), 4.
3. Thom S. Rainer, *The Bridger Generation* (Nashville: Broadman & Holman Publishers, 1997), 3.
4. George Barna, *Real Teens: A Contemporary Snapshot of Youth Culture* (Ventura, CA: Regal Books, 2001), 17.
5. Peter Jennings, *ABC World News Tonight*, December 19, 1997.
6. Neil Howe and William Strauss, *Millennials Rising: The Next Great Generation* (New York: Random House, 2000), 6.
7. Ibid., 7.
8. There is no consensus on the beginning or end of each generation. I have chosen to use the dates suggested by Neil Howe and William Strauss in their study of American generations. They are generally considered to be the experts and appear to have done the most research and writing on the subject.

William Strauss and Neil Howe, *Generations: The History of America's Future, 1584 to 2069* (New York: William Morrow and Company, Inc., 1991), 428.

Neil Howe and William Strauss, *Millennials Go to College: Strategies for a New Generation on Campus* (Washington: American Association of Collegiate Registrars and Admissions Officers and LifeCourse Associates, 2003), 19.

9. William Strauss and Neil Howe with Pete Markiewicz, *Millennials and the Pop Culture: Strategies for a New Generation of Consumers in Music, Movies, Television, the Internet, and Video Games* (LifeCourse Associates, 2006), 58-59.

10. "The Echo Boomers: Steve Kroft Reports On The Children Of The Baby Boomers," *CBSNews.com*, December 26, 2004, http://www.cbsnews.com/stories/2004/10/01/60minutes/main646890.shtml (accessed June 20, 2006).

11. Neil Howe and William Strauss, *Millennials Go to College: Strategies for a New Generation on Campus* (Washington: American Association of Collegiate Registrars and Admissions Officers and LifeCourse Associates, 2003), 51–42.

12. Daniel Egeler, *Mentoring Millennials: Shaping the Next Hero Generation* (Colorado Springs, NavPress, 2003), 32.

13. Claire Raines, "Managing Millennials," *Connecting Generations: The Sourcebook for a New Workplace* (Berkeley: Crisp Publications, 2003). Online at http://www.generationsatwork.com/articles/millenials.htm (accessed July 24, 2006).

14. Neil Howe and William Strauss, *Millennials Go to College: Strategies for a New Generation on Campus* (Washington: American Association of Collegiate Registrars and Admissions Officers and LifeCourse Associates, 2003), 11.

15. Ibid., 59.

16. Ibid.

17. George Barna, *Real Teens: A Contemporary Snapshot of Youth Culture* (Ventura, CA: Regal Books, 2001), 74.

18. Christian Smith with Melissa Lundquist Denton, *Soul Searching: The Religious and Spiritual Lives of American Teenagers* (New York: Oxford University Press, 2005), 56.

19. Ibid., 267.

20. George Barna, *Real Teens: A Contemporary Snapshot of Youth Culture* (Ventura, CA: Regal Books, 2001), 25.

21. "The Echo Boomers: Steve Kroft Reports On The Children Of The Baby Boomers," *CBSNews.com*, December 26, 2004, http://www.cbsnews.com/stories/2004/10/01/60minutes/main646890.shtml (accessed June 20, 2006).

22. Neil Howe and William Strauss, *Millennials Go to College: Strategies for a New Generation on Campus* (Washington: American Association of Collegiate Registrars and Admissions Officers and LifeCourse Associates, 2003), 57.

23. Leslie A. Goldgehn, "Generation Who, What Y? What You Need to

Know About Generation Y," *International Journal of Education Advancement* 5, no. 1, (April 8, 2004): 26.

24. Neil Howe and William Strauss, *Millennials Go to College: Strategies for a New Generation on Campus* (Washington: American Association of Collegiate Registrars and Admissions Officers and LifeCourse Associates, 2003), 123.

25. Daniel Egeler, *Mentoring Millennials: Shaping the Next Hero Generation* (Colorado Springs, NavPress, 2003), 37.

26. Neil Howe and William Strauss, *Millennials Rising: The Next Great Generation* (New York: Random House, 2000), 3.

27. George Barna, *Real Teens: A Contemporary Snapshot of Youth Culture* (Ventura, CA: Regal Books, 2001), 87.

28. Ibid., 61.

29. Walt Mueller, "Old Words for a New Culture," The Center for Parent/Youth Understanding, http://www.cpyu.org/Page.aspx?id=77199 (accessed June 20, 2006).

30. Christian Smith with Melissa Lundquist Denton, *Soul Searching: The Religious and Spiritual Lives of American Teenagers* (New York: Oxford University Press, 2005), 27.

31. Ibid., 44.

32. Thom S. Rainer, *The Bridger Generation* (Nashville: Broadman & Holman Publishers, 1997), 32.

33. Ron Hutchcraft, "Reaching the Global Youth Culture." Article available on a number of Web sites, including See You at the Pole: http://www.syatpaustralia.com/activate_details.cfm?id=20&version=normal. Accessed July 3, 2006.

DO YOU KNOW MORE THAN MY NAME?

Dwight Peterson

The results of the survey may have surprised some, but I antici-pated this precise outcome. Each semester, we ask our college youth ministry students to write a research paper on a youth ministry subject of their choice. In one of those assigned proj-ects, a student evaluated his own graduating class from a Chris-tian high school. He wanted to know where his fellow students were in their walks with God since graduation. What he found was alarming. Of the twenty-five students who graduated with him, twenty-one of them were no longer pursuing their walk with God.

After he concluded his presentation, I asked him how many of the twenty-one "shocked" him. He thought for a second and said, "I guess none of them really." In other words, he had no-ticed the warning signs that something was not right in their lives. I then asked him how many of those students knew that there were warning signs and what they were. He thought most of them probably felt like they were doing fine spiritually be-cause they were meeting the status quo.

When asked how many of those students had someone confront them with observations of warning signs, he could not think of anyone who had done so. This is the tragedy of many youth ministries. I wonder if those leaders who worked with these young people had remembered what James said, if things would not have been different. James admonishes us, "If one of you should wander from the truth and someone should bring him back, remember this: Whoever turns a sinner from the error of his way will save him from death and cover over a multitude of sins" (5:19–20 NIV).

One can only speculate what might have happened had solid spiritual diagnosis been going on within that ministry—how the lives of these kids may have been changed. What if there were diagnoses taken, observations made, and strategies formed to address the revealed issues? Perhaps a "multitude of sins" could have been covered, or perhaps (more accurately) uncovered. Maybe the apostle Paul's admonition of the "spiritual restoring" those overtaken by a fault (see Galatians 6:1) could have been effectively implemented.

"Spiritual diagnosis." When you read that term, what comes to your mind? Is it a lab overcoat and a dead body on a green gurney? Do you picture a pharisaical youth worker with his finger in your face telling you how ungodly you are? I hope you think of a loving, caring youth leader who takes time to discover the true needs in a young life.

When we think of spiritual diagnosis, we usually think of a judgmental attitude and seldom think of someone who is a loving or caring person. As a result, we seem to be doing little or no diagnosis in our ministries. Well, let me take that back. Just like the student who wrote the research project, we all do it. But we seldom respond to what we are seeing, or we feel guilty for "labeling" someone.

The concept of spiritual diagnosis evokes questions we need to address: Is spiritual diagnosis really a biblical concept? Should we be diagnosing others, or does it violate the biblical admonition to not judge? How can we do it effectively? Is there a difference between diagnosing and judging? Can we use this tool to rescue the students in our youth groups before they become statistics?

IS IT BIBLICAL TO MAKE SPIRITUAL DIAGNOSES?

The answer to the question is yes! It is not only a good idea, and helpful to the spiritual development of people, but it is the pattern of Scripture. Think about it. First, Jesus did it. In John 5:41–44, He told a group of people that they do not love God. How did He arrive at that conclusion? According to verse 44, it was because they sought praise from man but made no effort to obtain praise from God. In Matthew 7:15–20 Jesus gave a strong indictment, calling the Pharisees "ravenous wolves" among other things. How did He arrive at that conclusion? He looked at their fruit. In fact, He even called the people to examine the fruit of their teachers to determine if they should listen to them.

You might be saying, "Of course Jesus did it, but He was God. God does not need to look at an individual's fruit. He, as God, can look right into someone's heart. We can't." But Jesus was not the only one who did it. Paul also made spiritual diagnoses. In 1 Corinthians 3:1–4 he calls the Corinthians worldly, mere infants spiritually. He even tells them that his diagnosis had resulted in not being able to share a greater level of spiritual truth with them. Why did he come to this conclusion? He looked at their fruit. In Galatians 5, Paul provides a list of qualities for the Galatians to look for so they, too, would be able to make a spiritual diagnosis of others.

James, the brother of Jesus and an early church leader, made spiritual diagnoses. He defined what true religion looks like in James 1:26–27. He made the bold statement that if your life does not demonstrate tongue-control, mercy on the destitute, and holiness, you have a false religion. John does it in 1 John 2:3–6 when he tells us how to know if we, or others we know, are truly children of God. In fact, the entire epistles of James and 1 John are primarily devoted to helping people make spiritual diagnoses of their own lives and the lives of others.

WHY MAKE A SPIRITUAL DIAGNOSIS?

The first reason we need to make spiritual diagnoses is the condition and the deceptive tendencies of our hearts. In Jeremiah 17:9, we are told, "The heart is deceitful above all things and beyond cure. Who can understand it?" (NIV). In Matthew

7:21–23 we are told that there will be many people who think they have eternal life who, in fact, do not. Since we can be so easily deceived about the true condition of our lives, we need to be making honest, personal evaluations and diagnoses, as well as inviting others to examine our lives.

I remember when a young girl named Beccah began to attend our youth group and the local Christian school. Soon after she arrived, two other young ladies came to me concerned about what they saw in her life. They were concerned that she was not saved and did not have a genuine relationship with Christ. We prayed together and determined they ought to sit down with her and share their observations. Beccah's response was that she had made a decision when she was young, so she was already saved.

A year and a half later at our Winter Advance, the two girls came to us crying. They were still burdened for Beccah and the lack of spiritual fruit in her life. We prayed again, and I shared with them a passage of Scripture, which I thought would help them show her what her fruit might be indicating about her salvation. A few hours later, all three girls came back to us in tears, sharing with us that Beccah had trusted Christ. They didn't need to tell us though: it was all over her face. To this day, Beccah, a wife and mother of two, is thankful that two friends did spiritual diagnosis and shared their thoughts with her, leading to her salvation.

A second reason we need to be making spiritual diagnoses is because we want to help others grow spiritually. Hebrews 3:12–13 tells us that in order to avoid developing a sinful and unbelieving heart, we need to encourage each other daily. Galatians 6:1–5 tells us that those of us who are "spiritual" ought to help restore those who sin. Obviously, there must be some way to determine those who are spiritual and those who are caught in sin. James 5:19–20 tells us that if we see someone wandering from the truth, we ought to restore them. How do we know if they are wandering? We must make a spiritual diagnosis in the lives of others.

The third reason we ought to be making spiritual diagnoses is that Satan wants to destroy us (1 Peter 5:8). He will masquerade as an "angel of light" (2 Corinthians 11:13–14). Satan wants to deceive true believers, and we should use diagnosis as a preventative tool. When we see a friend moving in the wrong direction, we need to care enough to intervene. We need to share what we are seeing, not to accuse, but to confront tenderly.

Kathy was a sweet young girl in our youth group. The longer she dated her boyfriend, the more disturbed we became. But I was afraid to offend or hurt someone, so I said nothing. Each time I saw them, I grew more concerned. I knew what it was that concerned me, but I kept quiet. I can still feel the pain when the pastor told the deacons that he had gotten a call from Kathy's folks informing him that Kathy was pregnant. My heart sank. What if I had stepped in? What if I had had the courage to get involved and share my concerns? I determined that night never to allow my fears to keep me from being a brother in Christ willing not only to observe but also to love enough to share my concerns.

A final motivation for diagnoses is that we should desire the knowledge to be a help to those who need it. In Hebrews 5:11–14, the author told his audience where he saw them spiritually and what they needed to do in order to mature. In many of Paul's letters, 1 Corinthians 3:1–3 for example, he told his audience about their spiritual conditions. He then gave instruction to help them move forward. A spiritual diagnosis expands our opportunity for ministry. To help people, we need to determine where they are and what they need, and we should give them biblical guidelines and solutions.

WHAT DOES SPIRITUAL DIAGNOSIS REVEAL?

First, diagnosis can help reveal the spiritual condition of people. James 2:14 asks a sobering question: "Can faith save him?" James implies there are many kinds of faith, but only one that actually saves. Further, 1 John gives us indicators of true faith.

Salvation is not the only spiritual condition diagnosis reveals. It also reveals conditions like carnality. Paul makes it clear in 1 Corinthians 3:1–4 and Romans 7:14–20 that his diagnosis revealed the people to be in a carnal condition. Diagnosis can provide information about specific spiritual conditions that should help us help others take steps forward in their faith.

Jeff saw himself as a spiritual teen, ready for leadership. We saw him differently. One day at our Winter Advance, he came to a meal intentionally late, missed the serving line and consequently didn't get to eat. His poor response revealed the very issues we had hoped to help him see. Jeff had great potential to be a spiritual leader, but he needed to get beyond his carnality if he was going to be all that he could be.

Jeff would be the first to tell you how that confrontation affected his life in an unforgettable way. He went home anxious to do something about what he saw in his life. By God's grace he not only became a spiritual leader in our church, he also stepped it up at his high school, college, and now as the youth pastor in that same church.

Second, diagnosis reveals potential qualities necessary for ministry. Diagnosis should not be used as a negative, critical process. It not only reveals problems but also helps people see their strengths and how they can best be utilized for ministry. An example would be Paul in Romans 15:14, where his diagnosis revealed that the Romans were competent to instruct one another. Spiritual diagnosis helps people accomplish God's purpose for their lives.

Brian was a student I had known superficially for two years. Up until a wilderness trip, I had gotten nowhere with him. On Wednesday morning of our trip, we decided to have individual meetings with the guys before we sent them off for their solo time. As God would have it, Brian ended up speaking with me. As we reviewed his goal sheet, I asked him why he had listed weaknesses but no strengths. He shared that he could not think of any areas of strength in his life. When I pressed him, he then turned to me and said, "What do you think my strengths are?"

Thank God, I had done some diagnosis and was able to share with him what I had seen in his life. His life and our relationship was never the same. He walked out of the woods that week with a great desire to fulfill the promise God had given to him. Diagnosis had been the key to unlock the door of his heart.

WHAT DO WE LOOK FOR?

One area of surprise during my years in ministry has been how reluctant people are to engage in spiritual diagnosis. I have learned that people often feel as though it is wrong at worst and impossible at best to make a diagnosis of someone else's life. When I have occasion to talk about this subject, I will often begin with the question, "Is external behavior a true indicator of internal spiritual reality?" The most common answer is that external behaviors (what I can see) are not true indicators of internal spiritual reality (what I can't see). I have realized that most of us are looking at the wrong list of externals and are responding to what we see.

Students in many Christian colleges resist this issue because they have seen examples of others who looked spiritual but, over time, revealed that they were not. They are also concerned that some youth leaders put kids in prominent positions who are not living their faith behind the scenes! In fact, my wife Bonnie rejected Christianity early in her life because of the inconsistent Christianity she saw. She knew the kids who had prominent roles lived lives far from God.

These examples remind us that making spiritual diagnoses without using biblical standards will lead us to improper conclusions. Commonly we look at external activities such as participation in daily devotions, church ministries, and involvement in the youth group to give us clues. Since we all know teens who have faked us out, we are prone, and so are the teens, to question how we could ever make an effective spiritual diagnosis. The problem can be discovered in the external indicators we're looking for and using as our source. We find true biblical external indicators throughout Scripture. When we make a diagnosis based on these guidelines, we can get helpful and accurate readings of a spiritual reality.

For example, Galatians 5:19–26 provides us with a list of many indicators that we can see and that demonstrate an internal spiritual reality. You may be having your devotions regularly, but you cannot have joy, peace, patience, kindness, etc., if you are not truly saved. You may be involved in a ministry of your local church; but if there is idolatry, hatred, jealousy, rage, etc., in your life, then you are not walking in the Spirit.

Our church was sponsoring an outreach ministry using basketball. I had asked a number of our teens to recruit unsaved friends to play and to hear the gospel. Becky came to me with what she thought was a great idea for our outreach basketball league. She wanted to create a new area of ministry for kids who were not on teams. The plan was for them to walk around engaging in conversations with visitors and those who were not playing.

While this sounded like a great idea, the reality was that Becky thought she looked overweight in basketball shorts and was trying to find a way to get out of being on one of the teams. Her motivation revealed a spiritual need. If we looked at the wrong external indicators, we might have concluded she was making a very "godly" decision and noted her concern for others as a mature action. The truth was that she lived her life focused on herself, not on others or Christ.

Becky soon realized that this was not the only time she made such decisions. She later confessed that she could not remember one decision she ever made to please God that cost her personally. The Spirit of God used this seemingly insignificant incident to show Becky she was far from being a spiritual girl. She faced the truth and trusted Christ; her salvation changed her life.

A couple of years later, I received a phone call late one night from Becky. She was on a ministry team at her college and explained how she had participated in an outreach event that night. The event involved an obstacle course with food, mud, and a variety of other messy creations. At the end of the evening she turned to the kids who were all laughing and told me she thought to herself, *If only Dwight could see me now!* Her focus has shifted from her needs to others' needs.

We must develop, possess, and use the skills that will enable us to spot both positive and negative manifestations of the biblical indicators. As we observe them, we must be quick to respond to what we see. Our response should correct what is wrong and encourage spiritual fruit. Let's think about diagnosis in specific spiritual categories.

Natural Man (Unsaved)

The Bible clearly reveals the characteristics of one who is unsaved. First Corinthians 2:14 tells us that the unsaved cannot accept spiritual truth. Second Corinthians 4:4 tells us that Satan has blinded the minds of the unsaved. So how would a student who does not understand the Bible behave in youth group? He may be disruptive, but he also may be polite. Because he does not know Christ, he does not understand the truths you are teaching. When he does participate in youth group discussions, he demonstrates that he has missed the point.

The natural man shows no evidence of God at work in his life. According to Hebrews 12, there is no discipline from God present in his life. One of the ways we recognize a child of God is God's discipline in his life. If God is not revealing sin, we can assume that he is not saved until proven otherwise. We must look for evidence that God is revealing sin and confronting him with it.

Carnal Man (Infant)

According to 1 Corinthians 3:1–2, the carnal man still has his loyalties fixed on a human scale. He is beginning to care about what God thinks, but he is still more concerned about what people think. Hebrews 5:12—6:3 shows how the carnal man struggles with "meat," which symbolizes God's kind of righteousness. "Meat" is the ability to understand how biblical truth applies to life. It is progressing from a truth that I simply accept intellectually to an understanding of how that truth affects the way I live.

The carnal student may choke when you address how the truth impacts his life. He can be defensive when you challenge him in specific areas of his life. You may hear him overreact to a discussion on Philippians 4:8 by saying something like, "I guess we should all throw out our TVs and live in a cave somewhere!"

In relation to sin, Galatians 5 tells us that the carnal man lives according to a list. He feels that any behavior not forbidden in Scripture is fine, or he creates a list of what is right and defines his spirituality by that list. He might ask questions like, "Is it wrong if I . . ." or, "Is it a sin to watch. . . ." He is not motivated by righteousness but by staying on the right side of the line.

Spiritual Man (Adolescent)

The spiritual man is motivated by pleasing God. His loyalties are not with people but with God. He is not as moved by peer pressure and is able to stand against the crowd, knowing his behavior pleases his heavenly Father. In fact, he often defends what is right, although his position makes him look foolish to the world. See 1 Corinthians 2:15–16 and 1 John 4:7–21.

He is not as concerned about whether an activity is sinful; instead, he wants to know its benefit—if it will help him in his pursuit of righteousness (2 Timothy 2:22). He wants to know if it will help him reach his unsaved friends for Christ (1 Corinthians 10:33). For the spiritual man, life is not about the lists but about his relationships. He might ask diagnostic questions like, "What will happen if I. . . ." He is willing to question those things which slow him down and lay them aside (Hebrews 12:1–2). He wants to put on the armor of God in order to take a stand against Satan.

HOW DO WE RESPOND IN OUR DIAGNOSIS?

First, we must minister to our students on their spiritual levels. Paul tells us in 1 Thessalonians 5:14 (NIV), "And we urge you, brothers, warn those who are idle, encourage the timid, help the weak, be patient with everyone." Obviously, if we are to respond properly to the idle, the timid, or the weak, we must make spiritual diagnoses to know their categories. It will not help the weak to warn them or to encourage them. In some cases, we do not help, and we hurt their spiritual progress.

Paul also tells us in Galatians 6:1–2 (NIV), "Brothers, if someone is caught in a sin, you who are spiritual should restore him gently. But watch yourself, or you also may be tempted. Carry each other's burdens, and in this way you will fulfill the law of Christ." Again, we can't know who is caught in a sin or who is burdened, if we are not making a spiritual diagnosis. If we want to be able to minister to people and be helpful to them, then we must begin by addressing the needs of individuals where they presently are.

A spiritual diagnosis is not judgment or condemnation. This type of superior attitude is what may have led believers to be intolerant and unkind, or afraid to confront real sin issues in the church today. Some of you may have been hurt by the labels people have placed on you based on their diagnosis. Matthew 7:1–2 makes it clear that we are not to judge. Luke 18:11–14 tells us the story of the tax collector and the Pharisee praying; we must be like the tax collector. We must never forget our own sinfulness and our need for a Savior. We are making diagnoses with a desire to be helpful and a desire to see people grow, not to demonstrate our superiority or have a critical spirit. We need to become burdened *for* people, not frustrated *with* people.

GEAR UP FOR TRUE SUCCESS!

Having a ministry that addresses the spiritual needs of students is a sobering task and an immense responsibility. Being called of God to influence the lives of teenagers is hard and scary. We don't want to devote years of our lives to a task to which God has called us—and have nothing to show for it. A friend once gave me a quote that is still on display in my office:

> My greatest fear in life is not that I will be a failure, but that I will be highly successful at that which does not matter.

We may be successful at being liked and even loved by our students. We might be highly successful in the numbers game of youth ministries. We may be highly successful and well on the way to becoming the next youth ministry guru. But all that really matters is the spiritual impact we have in the lives of people. Do the teens I work with know God more intimately because of my influence? Are they growing to be more like Christ? Are they confessing sin? Are they reaching their worlds?

God has called us to a monumental task. But He has empowered us with His Spirit and equipped us with His Word. His Word not only calls us to make spiritual diagnoses, it guides our diagnoses. We must grow in our knowledge and then in our skill to diagnose the needs of people and minister to those needs. Only then can we truly be successful at that which matters! Only then might we change the numbers that really count—one at a time!

GO WHERE THEY ARE

Tim Ahlgrim

Not long after I arrived in a new ministry and city, I made my first visit to the local high school campus. I wore my usual conservative ministry costume of sport coat, tie, and (since it was winter) my best trench coat. While students were at lunch, I walked through the cafeteria looking for a teacher. I walked from one end to the other, went out in the hall and back through the cafeteria again. I never found the person I was searching for, but I did discover an amazing thing! Several students from my youth group were in the cafeteria that day. I saw them, they saw me, but we never spoke or publicly acknowledged each other. I had what I thought was a good reason for not speaking. I did not want to embarrass them. However, I was stunned that they didn't recognize me. Maybe it was the trench coat! Later that night in youth group at church, three kids came up to me and said, "Pastor Tim, you will never believe what happened in school! There was a guy who walked through the cafeteria today who looked almost like you!" We all had a laugh when I told them it was me. At the end of the discussion, they asked me a question that set me on a course of action for my ministry to this day. They asked me, "Pastor Tim, why would you ever want to be in our school?" The students I worked with could think of no reason why I should be in their school.

This forced me to think of why I would want to be in their school. What was the best way to be involved while I was there? How could I get involved? After seriously considering these questions, I arrived at several conclusions.

THE MISSION FIELD

One of the greatest mission fields for anyone who works with students must be the public school. When we desire to influence the world for Christ, schools in our own communities are a good place to begin. As the burden and passion for foreign mission and ministry are gaining in popularity, I would like to return attention to students in our own communities. It is true that around 95 percent of teenagers in the world do not live in the United States. This increases the need for international youth ministry. According to Cheryl Fawcett and Dave Patty of the Josiah Project, it may also be true that of the teenagers living in America, 90 percent of them do not know Christ as their Savior. We can do visitation, Bible studies, worship, or special events, but we will never encounter so many students all in one place as in the schools. American students must not become a neglected mission field.

THE SCRIPTURES

Beginning with Acts 1:8, Jesus gives us, at the very least, geographical guidance about our witness for Him. "But you shall receive power when the Holy Spirit has come upon you; and you shall be witnesses to Me in Jerusalem, and in all Judea and Samaria, and to the end of the earth." Simply stated, the listeners knew that Jerusalem was their hometown. They were to be His witnesses in the place where they lived first. It seems that after our hometown witness, we are then to move outward and eventually be witnesses for Christ in faraway lands. In the excitement of jumping to international missions, we often neglect the first obligation of our "Jerusalem." We must not forget that this includes the local school system.

Matthew 5:13–16 is a second passage significant to local school ministry. Jesus says emphatically that those of us who follow Him are the "salt of the earth" and the "light of the world." The application of Matthew 5 is helpful in considering ministry to the public school. There is a strong cultural and religious view that the public school is not safe, not giving students a quality education, and not compatible with the teaching of the church. Since the 1960s in the United States, communities, organizations, and churches look for and provide ways to educate their children apart from the public school. In some cases, this is necessary. In other cases, alternative schools are started for less than noble reasons like fear, racism, and elitism.

The consequence of turning from the public schools is present in our culture. Over these forty years, many Christians withdrew their children from the public schools and turned toward private Christian schools. Christian education is a good thing, but it may have contributed inadvertently to the decline in public education. Both sides of the public and private school issue can be argued in convincing fashion, but that is not the purpose here. What is not debatable is that when Christians leave anything, for whatever reason, what remains will always be worse than if Christians were present. This seems like a perfect place for salt and light to be used for Christ!

In Jesus' day, salt had a couple of primary functions. The first was to flavor meat, and the second was to slow the decay of meat. Christians have a flavoring influence in the public school just like salt flavors meat. Salt flavors by highlighting the taste of meat. A person wants to eat the meat because of the taste enhancement capabilities of salt. When we are being salt in the culture, people with whom we come into contact will want to know more about Christ because we salt, or flavor, the culture with Him.

I saw this principle illustrated one day when the head of security at the high school asked me what the difference was between the students he knew and some students he didn't know. As head of security, he only knew kids who got into trouble around the school. The students he asked me about stayed out of trouble, said hello to him, and even wished him a good day! When he told me their names, I was able to tell him the difference: these kids knew Christ as their Savior, and their relationship with the risen Savior caused him to notice their radically different behavior. These *salty* students were flavoring the hallways of their high school!

Salt also preserved the meat or slowed its decay. This was the "freezer" of Jesus' time. People would rub salt into the meat and it would slow the spoilage and decay, helping to preserve it. Jesus was saying that, as salt in the culture, His followers would slow the decay in the culture.

As a wrestling coach, I would get ready for practice in the coaches' locker room that doubled as our offices. Every day when I arrived, the coach whose desk was closest to the door would yell at the top of his lungs, "Howdy, Reverend." I was embarrassed because I knew he was notifying the other coaches that I had arrived. With his two-word greeting, he was telling the staff to stop swearing, telling off-color jokes, and in general, behave because "the reverend" was here! I didn't like being singled out until I realized that Christ's prescription of salt was doing its job. I was a preservative. Because I was in the room, cultural decay in the form of bad language, jokes, and behavior slowed or ceased for that day. If I wasn't in the room, there was nothing to check their behavior. Salt was doing its job and delayed the decay of the culture when I arrived!

The application to believers in the public school is significant. When Christians are present in the school, because of the nature of salt, it will be a better place. Conversely, when we are not present, there may be nothing to slow the decay. In the last half century, we have seen the harmful results of fewer believers in the schools. Many times, the quality of education and character of the culture have gone in a negative direction.

The second emphatic fact in Matthew 5:13–16 is that we are "light." We must let our lights shine. A light is most effective in the darkness. People are drawn to the light shining in the darkness. We reflect the light of Christ. They will be drawn to us because we have something they do not have. We have the abundant life that Christ gives, and we reflect that fact in every area of our lives. I know of two students who were on one of

the school's athletic teams. They were also part of the same local church youth ministry. They did not know it at the time,
but a teammate had been watching them for two years. He
knew something was different about them. Finally, he heard the
good news of Jesus that had changed their lives and could
change his. After he became a believer, he told about watching
his friends and knowing he wanted what they had. He was at-
tracted to the light in their lives and became a believer himself.
The basic problem with most Christians today may be that we
are never in the darkness. Because of that fact, our light is not
shining as Christ intended.

To be a light that is drawing people to Christ and the salt
that preserves and flavors the culture, we must understand two
key facts. The first is that light is only effective where it is dark.
How many of us are lights in a dark place? The second fact is
that salt is only effective if it is where there is evil. To light the
culture and slow the decay of culture, light and salt must be
where it is dark and evil! The question is where is the best place
for salt and light to be utilized? The school needs salt; otherwise, evil will have its way. The school needs light; otherwise,
the darkness will overwhelm it. It seems to me that the school
is an awesome place to utilize the characteristics of salt and
light! This is why Christians need to be there.

As we read these concepts, many of us recoil from salt and
light because of teaching that says we should not be present
where there is darkness and evil. We are fearful that if we encourage our students to do this, then they will not be able to resist the temptation of a dark world. I am confident that since
God's Word is true, Christians will influence the culture. We do
not need to fear that our students will be swallowed up by the
culture. We are salt, and we are light. We can be nothing else. I
agree with G. K. Chesterton who said that beef and salt will
never be the same. Beef is beef, and salt is salt. The reason salt
seasons so well is not because it is like beef, but because it is so
entirely different from beef. In the same way, our students who
know Christ will be salt and light, not because they are like the

world, but because they are so entirely different from the world! In the school, they will be the salt of the earth and the light of the world.

THE CHURCH

The church is God's mechanism to reach the world. The better the church does its job, the more Christ will influence the culture and the more the church will influence the school. Youth workers in the church need to discover a doorway of opportunity for people who enter their youth ministry for the first time. An effective local church ministry will provide a springboard into the school as well an oasis for students. This is the first area of work and concern.

The church can be a tool for the public school and therefore intentionally build a supportive relationship with the school. In larger cities, there are minority families and students. The school is always on the lookout for minority adults and older students who have used the opportunity for success that an education provides. The church can help to locate and recommend individuals for the school. Another avenue to minister to the community and school is for the church to have a class on parenting as part of its Christian education program. Teaching parents the biblical principles of parenting will strengthen the school and the church ministry that has targeted the school. A church that trains and provides mentors for students will be effective in many communities. Students from difficult home situations, single-parent families, or latchkey homes will all benefit from a mentor. A mentor from the church youth ministry can be greatly used by the Lord in the school.

The church's student ministry program also can be a tool to reach students in the community and school. Youth workers should intentionally build an aspect of the ministry to reach students who don't normally attend your church. For example, once a month we would have what we called "Friday Night

Live." This was an activity designed to reach students with the gospel. It was always different; it always included a gospel presentation; it was not always on Friday night. The students in our group knew that when this event was on the schedule they were to bring their friends to hear the gospel. Another program idea is planning special events when unusual things happen to students and the community. We do memorial services when a student dies. This brings many people to hear the gospel. It also puts people on notice that our church is interested in them. There may be as many ideas as there are churches. The issue I am raising is this: to reach students in the community and schools, the church must do something!

Another point should be made from the local church point of view. Sometimes, youth workers operate from a position of antagonism toward the school. They are committed to combating what they think are the negative aspects of the public school and use their ministry as the weapon of choice. Examples include "anti-homecoming" or "anti-prom" events. Some of us may have had "alternative" events on our calendar. I know a youth worker who even tried to schedule an assembly in the school that would have presented a viewpoint counter to what was being taught in class. This view of the school causes tension in our ministry by forcing the students to make unnecessary choices. It also creates an image in the community that will not bear good fruit in school ministry.

The prom is an example of church youth workers potentially shooting themselves in the foot. It is such a big event in my city that while the prom is in progress, people form a line around the school at 10 p.m. that night. Several thousand people from the community pay a couple of dollars for a ticket that allows them entrance to the gymnasium balcony at 11 p.m. From the upper bleachers, people can watch the "Grand March." The Grand March, quite simply, is when the seniors take three laps around the gym. People pay good money to watch the kids walk three times around the gym! The principal presents the senior class to the community, everyone cheers, and parents cry! As a youth worker, that is a place I want to be! It would be counterproductive in my community to present an alternative event to the prom. It might occupy a few students who are not seniors, but I definitely would limit my opportunity to influence students and families for Christ! The youth worker with a bent toward antagonism and competition with the public school will not have a prolonged impact with students. An effective outreach ministry to the school must begin with the church, its programs, and a positive view of the community and school.

THE COMMITMENT

As we consider ministry in the public school, we must decide what our commitment level will be. Our view of school ministry will certainly vary according to the amount of time we are able to commit to it. We will be successful with our ministry to the school in proportion to our commitment to the school. This does not mean that you must commit a great deal of time and energy, nor does it mean you fully agree with the humanistic orientation of the public school system as a whole, but it **does** mean that you must commit to the ministry itself. We should become a fixture at whatever school activities we can attend. If we are seldom seen during the school year, we will in all probability accomplish nothing. We must, at some level, commit to the school.

One youth pastor in town is a girls' soccer coach and a soccer official. In the fall, he assumes a high level of commitment. His commitment is seasonal and spans the girls' soccer season. Another youth pastor tries to eat lunch with kids at the school that has an open campus one time per month. Eating lunch takes less time than coaching soccer, but his level of commitment is similar. He is serious about being at the school one time each month. We must decide what we want to accomplish, the amount of commitment we are able and willing to give, and then follow through.

THE GOAL

Perhaps the most important aspect of working in the schools is for us to answer the question, "What is our goal for wanting to be there?" Our goal must be similar to that of the school if we will gain an entrance. Every school administrator and teacher desires that the school be successful in its mission. My goal in working with them is to help them to be successful. When I introduce myself to them, I even express my desire to help make them successful at what they do. We must gain trust by serving the school selflessly.

A step we must take in an effort to achieve this goal is the step of prayer. We should pray for the staff and the students of the school. It is a good idea to let the school staff know that we are praying for their success. If you pray for me, you will demonstrate that you care about me, and therefore I will respond to you in a way that corresponds with your expression of love for me. Your prayer for me makes a difference. The same is true with the school administration. When you pray for them and their success in their jobs, they will respond to you in a positive way. A group of youth workers informed several school administrators that we were praying for them. We asked them if they had specific concerns that we could take to the Lord on their behalf. One high school principal asked us to pray that he would have wisdom as he makes decisions throughout the day. He wanted wisdom to deal with every student, parent, and decision he needed to make on the job. This principal now has a group of youth workers praying for his success as he wisely deals with the everyday decisions.

We should consider some caution as we think about our goals for working in the school. Many times I have seen youth workers venture toward school ministry and end up totally out of the school loop. There are some good reasons for this lack of success. At the core of the failure are faulty goals on the part of youth workers. The first faulty goal grows from a viewpoint of antagonism toward the school. We may have the idea that the school is a secular indoctrination factory. We put our effort into the goal of saving the culture. We therefore see ourselves as the champions of truth who will set the record straight. This antagonistic goal will not work. The second faulty goal is the goal of growing the attendance in your group and church. A result of your being in the school may be numerical growth, but it cannot be your primary goal. This goal will not work for you either. The final faulty goal to consider is a pitfall for those of us who are young and still full of energy. We may strive to work in the school to showcase whatever skills we may have. This goal comes from immaturity. We seek to be in the limelight, and sometimes we do what it takes to keep ourselves there. Even if we are able to pull this one off, this goal will not last very long. The staff of the school is smarter than that. By the way, your church staff is smarter than that too!

The school staff will see through any goal or agenda we have that is different from the one they have for themselves. We must work in the school for their success. God will bring success to us, but our success must not be our primary goal. If it is, this ministry will not work.

THE RESULTS

Another goal-related question is what result do we want to see from this relationship with the school and its students? Ultimately, the salvation of students, staff, and teachers is at the heart of everything we do. Our group has seen students receive Christ. Our church has seen families attend as a result of our presence in the school. These results are great, but they are not the primary result that we will see.

One result we should be always looking for is that of influence. When I work with students in the community, kids and families are influenced by the gospel. When families have needs, influence will be the reason they call me. When a wrestler became a Christian, his family began to come to church to see what was behind the change in their son. They came to our church to find out what was happening because someone from our church was working with their son on the team. That influence drew them. A student in the community was tragically killed in an accident. Because the family was aware of their son's contact with our youth pastor, they called him to do the funeral. His influence with students in that school resulted in several hundred students and staff hearing the gospel at the funeral. A good fact to remember about communities, schools, and parents is this: when we love their kids, they will love us. If influence is a primary result of your goal, you will be encouraged as it grows and opens doors to the gospel and further ministry. I have been to graduations, weddings, and dinners with families simply because of the influence built by my taking time with their kids.

THE PLAN

There needs to be a deliberate and methodological process when we decide to work in the public school. We must have a plan that includes introduction, observation, and participation. How will we meet school staff and teachers? How will we know about the school and the important student activities? How much are we willing to commit to participating in school ministry? These are questions that we must consider and answer if we will have effective ministries in the public schools.

Introduction

What is the best way to meet the staff of the middle or high school that is most influential in my church and youth ministry? We should take purposeful steps to meet the staff. If I am new in town or new to the school ministry, my first effort is to meet the principal and administrators of the school. Make an appointment with the principal and keep it. Look him or her in the eye and explain that you work with students at your church, so you wanted to meet him. Tell him that it is your desire to work in an effective way with the students in the same community where he works. Let him know that you are willing to help in any way he thinks you could. Ask if there is any aspect of his job in which you might help him. Let him know that you will be praying for him as he daily works with students, teachers, and families in the community. Along with introducing yourself and the ministry to the principal and staff at the school, you must observe the activities of the school.

Observation

It also is a good idea to observe the place of the high school in the community. Two questions should be answered. First, what is going on at the high school and in the lives of students? And second, how much influence does the high school and its activities have on the community as a whole? In order to find out about activities, you need to use all of your senses. You must think outside of the church and your office walls. You should be reading the newspaper, watching the local news and sports, and listening to the radio.

On the first weekend I was in my city, I noticed how much TV time was given to girls' basketball. Every score and highlight was announced for the girls' teams. They even included small-town teams. I found this strange since girls' basketball wasn't given that kind of attention where I came from. It only took me a couple of days to conclude that in my new community girls' basketball was important. As a new member of the community, I now had a decision to make. Do I ignore what I have learned, or do I figure out how to use the new information as a springboard for ministry? I chose the latter. A couple of years later, I had some students in my youth group who were members of the state girls' basketball championship team. Not only was I able to attend a ballgame or two, but I was also able to speak intelligently with the girls about their season. I learned about their school activity, and I was able to make their athletic achievement part of the youth ministry at church.

Communicate with students and parents. Find out what is going on outside the church by asking. I would personally ask for information, teach the volunteer staff to seek information, and even have the kids fill out a form that would tell us what they were doing and when they were doing it. Another way to learn is the media. Read the newspaper. In fact, the only reason I subscribe to the paper is to read about the high school's activities. In the normal sports page, you can find the results of activities. Second, an important part of our paper is what I call the "small print page." Every paper has one of these. It is the place where the box scores are printed. Sometimes the only place a student's name shows up is in the box score on the small print page. This page also tells what is happening today and this week. A peek in today's paper tells me there are a JV football game, a guys' soccer game, and a tennis match. I can organize my time and catch some of the students in action. A final benefit to knowing about school activities is that the youth worker from my church (me) is seen at the school and its events. People become familiar with me because I show interest in their students.

Use this information as a point of affirmation and contact in your ministry. Send kids and teams a note including a copy of the article. Pat students on their backs and give them encouragement for their dedication, results, or effort.

Finding out the school's influence on the community may take a little more time. We need to be observing other programs and extra-curricular activities during the school year. How does the community feel about the school? How does the community support events sponsored by the school? Where is the influence of the school felt in the community? Do people support the music program? Answering one or more of these questions will help determine the influence of the school. The music program is huge in the school where I work. If I am to minister to students in my area, I must know about the music department. The marching band competes on the state level and travels to holiday parades around the country. This demonstrates a high level of commitment by a large number of students and families. There are several hundred students who participate in seven concert and show choirs. At Christmas and in the spring, the choirs perform for the community. The community fills a two thousand-seat theater five times over the course of a weekend for these concerts and, at seven dollars a seat, the community demonstrates their commitment to the school. I need to know about and attend these events in order to minister effectively in the community.

Start practicing the art of observation, and increase your influence in the local school.

Participation

I believe there are two ways to participate in the schools. I call these, for lack of a better name, "direct participation" and "indirect participation." Indirect participation is more passive and perhaps a way to get acquainted with the school as we use our time. Direct participation is more hands-on. Indirect participation may not even require you to enter the school building. Direct participation will cause you to be present in the school and at events.

Indirect participation can be the doorway to the public school. It is in this level of participation that everyone can and should participate. It grows from an alert awareness of what is happening in the schools and community. You do not have to be involved by having an on-site physical presence, an extraordinary investment of time, or a great familiarity with the school. Indirect participation will lead to those things though! You can be involved in this way by paying attention to the newspaper, television, and radio in your area. When you hear of or see a student, staff member, or teacher accomplish good things, be sure and write a note of congratulation.

I learned the incredible lessons of indirect participation while I served as a volunteer high school wrestling coach. Our team won the city championship, and a couple of days later a letter from the mayor was posted on our bulletin board in the locker room. Our head coach read the letter, looked at me, and said, "I don't know anything about that guy, but he has my vote!" The mayor's interest in our school and team earned him two votes that day. It did not take me, as a young youth pastor, very long to figure out that there may be a local church application here! I began to keep my eyes and ears open and write letters or notes of congratulation. A few years later when my son began to have articles written about him, he would get letters of congratulation from our state senator. The senator went a step further, which gave me another idea. He would include a copy of the article with the note. I learned another nice touch in indirect participation, and the senator also has another loyal voter!

Are you beginning to see the value of indirect school participation? We should get into the habit of reading the box scores on the sports page and noticing the accomplishments of teachers. Just today I sent a note to the winning field goal kicker in Friday night's football game, complimented the coach on his team's off-season work which paid off in the game, and sent an e-mail to the soccer coach. It isn't even lunch time yet! Send the note to the student at the school in care of the coach. This is the best way to get through channels, and it also lets at least three individuals know that you are interested in the success of what they are doing. One important point not to overlook is that there are students who achieve great things off the athletic field and outside the gymnasium. Find a way to get on that information pipeline, too. Our local school keeps the top fifty academic seniors' photographs in a trophy case. It would be great for a youth worker in town to intentionally contact these students with an encouragement letter. Many colleges and universities have contacted them, but so far, no youth worker has. I know because my daughter is one of the top fifty! Send notes and letters and e-mails to establish an indirect participation in the schools.

The second type of participation is direct participation, and it requires a more physical presence in the school. Begin this type of participation by attending events at the school and then volunteering for involvement in an area where your passion lies. If you have a unique skill or expertise, offer yourself to the school.

I work in the athletic department. I participated on college wrestling and baseball teams; therefore, these are the sports where I volunteered. Initially my offer was rejected, but a couple of weeks later the coach gave me a call and accepted my offer to help coach. I also volunteered to coach a summer baseball team for middle school students. The two summers on the ball diamond continue to pay dividends. People still recognize me because of the time I spent with their children! I have a youth pastor friend who works with the yearbook and newspaper staff. He learned that the high school did not have anyone on staff with the knowledge and skill to work with the computer programs that print the school newspaper and yearbook. He offered to be a resource for the yearbook and newspaper staff and has become their main resource. Another youth pastor I know was a springboard diver throughout college. He learned that the diving coach was taking an educational leave and the team needed a coach. He volunteered to fill the vacancy. His ministry is still reaping the results of that season as the diving coach!

Volunteering may be the best way to gain access to your school. This direct participation will take time and commitment, but if God leads you to this front-line ministry, you will find room in your schedule. Volunteer on a consistent basis. Be dependable and efficient when you volunteer. If the school depends on you, be responsible for the reputation of the Lord and be dependable.

Direct and indirect participation are the two ways to be involved in your school. To be effective youth workers in our communities, we will need to be indirectly involved at least. One may lead to the other and allow God to give you great impact in the schools.

Here are a few guidelines as you participate in school ministry. You will need to convince your pastor and church board of the value of gaining influence in the school. Be diligent and go through the proper channels. You will need to put important school events on your calendar. As much as you can, if your students participate, put their activities on the church calendar. Remember that you are earning the right to influence students. Your ability and opportunity to share the gospel will probably be in proportion to the amount of influence you gain because of your dedication to the school ministry.

THE CONCLUSION

Jesus tells us that we are the "salt of the earth" and the "light of the world." We take mission trips around the world but may be failing in our own community. Let's retool and put the process in motion to return to Christ's formula of evangelism. Your Jerusalem, the local schools, probably could use some salt and light! Have a fruitful and exciting ministry working with students in their schools!

HOW TO BE INVOLVED IN THE SCHOOL

Here is an idea list that will jumpstart your thinking as to how you can be involved in public school ministry. The list grows from indirect to direct participation and is not exhaustive, but it can be used to start you thinking about your possible involvement in the school.

INDIRECT PARTICIPATION

Write letters to:

Congratulate teachers who win scholarships, awards, or grants.
Commend teachers for their work with students.
Commend school administrators for their work with students.
Commend students for accomplishment in scholastics, music, art, and athletics.
Let students and teachers know you are praying for them.

DIRECT PARTICIPATION

Attend:

Be a regular at games, concerts, news conferences, and banquets.
Become a fan of the school and students.

Experience:

Accidents, funerals, weddings, and sports injuries.

Volunteer:

Help in the cafeteria.
Counsel.
Chaperoning dances, proms, or after-prom events.
Coach.
Become an official/referee.
Help with the yearbook or school newspaper.
Volunteer in the library.
Help with clubs, e.g. fencing team, chess club, debate team, and Fellowship of Christian Athletes.
Make hospital visits.

Staff:

When they depend on you, they may hire you!

PUBLIC SCHOOL MINISTRY TOP 10 LIST

1. Be convinced that the school is a great mission field that needs you as salt and light.
2. Understand you are the salt of the earth and the light of the world.
3. Get started by praying for the school and staff.
4. Always have the success of the school be your first goal: participate directly and indirectly in the school.
5. Do not assume an adversarial point of view with the school. They have some of the same goals for students as you have.
6. Be sure to work under the authority of your pastor and church. School ministry will take a commitment of time and energy, so they should count the time you spend there as work hours.
7. Volunteer where your passion is.
8. Be alert to the events of student life as a point of contact, e.g. funerals, accidents, weddings, etc.
9. Consider **influence** as your prime result.
10. Get busy and influence your community for Christ by working in the school.

MORE THAN COOKIES AND PUNCH

Eric Hystad

It seemed to be a great idea at the time. All I had to do was round up students of all makes and models, convince them that their lives would not be complete without being a part of my event, lock them up at the church for twelve hours, order pizza, and prepare a "can't miss" Bible study that would convince them of their need for Christ—and quite possibly cause some to go to the mission field!

As a young youth pastor trying to balance college work and the responsibilities of ministry, I was swept up in trying to pull off an "event for the ages"! Though I was young and somewhat naïve about ministry, I knew one thing for sure: for me to be successful, I had to do events and activities, and the bigger the better. I wish I could say "the rest of the story" was positive. The truth is that those twelve hours seemed to last forever. Nobody told me it was a mistake to start your lock-in at 7:00 p.m. or that students would get bored easily. I never imagined that they would rebel when we put a two-slice limit on their pizza intake or that a powerful message about Jesus at 3:00 a.m. would be just another sleepy talk!

I learned a great deal from my very first youth ministry event. But even with less-than-spectacular results, I saw clearly the value of the "big event" in the process of doing youth work. For months after that lock-in, students would refer to those hours spent together and would quickly ask the inevitable question: "When are we going to do another one?" I watched as Jim and Jerry, twin brothers who prayed to receive Christ during the lock-in, continued to come to youth group and began to get serious about their faith. Their excitement for the Lord was contagious to the other students in our ministry, and these two young men helped give us credibility with other students. Even with the memories of the "pain and agony" throughout the night that would not end, I was sold! Christ-centered, purposeful, big events have been a staple of my ministry ever since.

A MARRIAGE MADE IN HEAVEN!

Far too many youth pastors make the mistake of "choosing sides." Some will point proudly to the number of students who attend their Bible study, have a consistent devotional life, read their Bible, and above all aren't messing around with the things "of the world." Their goal is to build disciples, and that is certainly a worthy objective! For them, evangelism is an afterthought, something that happens as a natural result of their "program." As their students grow and become more entrenched in the group, they will bring friends with them. This cycle continues to build the "group" with very little intentional evangelism occurring. On the other side of the fence, there are those who have never seen an event that they didn't like! Their passion is to see students saved, and the quickest way to make this happen is by invading their lives with events they cannot ignore. The front door is wide open as students are "invited in" to a relationship with Christ. The tragedy for many youth pastors is that the back door is as wide open as the front! With very little effort put into the training and development of their students, these ministries serve as "one-hit wonders" and quickly lose touch with the students who have been "reached" at these events.

The good news is that many youth pastors have recognized that a strong and purposeful discipleship program can co-exist with a well-planned and exciting event strategy. This can be a marriage made in heaven! Students who have only been exposed to the "holy huddle" of their youth groups find it incredibly challenging and exciting to get out of their comfort zone and reach other students. It is certainly a major stretch for them when they realize what it takes to touch the lives of some of their friends. At the same time, there is nothing so affirming as seeing a student get plugged into a relationship with Christ after coming to one of your events.

In early 2000, our church decided to hold an evangelistic event called Judgment House. It was to be held in October of that year and would be a walk-through drama portraying the realities of life, death, and eternity. This idea wasn't new, and it certainly didn't originate with us. Our goal was simple and direct. We wanted to introduce young and old to Jesus Christ! After months of team meetings and preparation, many late nights spent building sets, and last-minute worrying about lighting and sound, the event finally happened. We were somewhat surprised when more than ten thousand people made their way through the halls of our church, and ecstatic when over 1,300 of them made first-time decisions for Christ!

The "icing on the cake" was the results of that week in the lives of those who had made commitments to Christ. A friend of Judgment House had invited Azzie, a highly recruited football player in the Houston area. Not sure what he was getting into, Azzie gathered a bunch of his friends and made his way to the church. Watching and hearing the message of the play, he gave his life to Christ. A follow-up phone call, a letter or two encouraging him to visit our church, and Azzie was on his way! He began to grow in his faith and soon saw his own opportunity to share Christ with his friends. Azzie saw a number of guys on his team come to Christ in the months following Judgment House. This event was the catalyst for the incredible change in his life! Today Azzie continues to walk with the Lord; and though he is knee-deep in the challenging world of Division I college football, Azzie continues to influence others.

PARADISE AND PITFALLS

Planning an event that makes a difference for eternity is hard work. In my early years of ministry, I was encouraged to join the "once a month" club. I was reminded that every student wanted and deserved at least one youth group event a month. I just knew that this was commanded in some "how to be successful in youth ministry" book. My life soon revolved around those monthly calendar dates. Whether or not I could define any purpose behind these events wasn't important as long as we had something for these kids! It didn't take long for the joy to turn to discouragement and the creativity well to dry up. These events began as opportunities to reach out to others but soon drifted inward as our energy and enthusiasm waned, and they eventually became activities that served the saints.

At the very time I was getting pretty cynical about the whole idea of youth ministry, a wise friend in our church took me aside and reminded me of the old adage, "quality over quantity." He challenged me to rethink my strategy and to judge what I was doing in terms of eternal impact in the lives of students and adults alike. His encouraging words motivated me enough to make a change in how I planned and scheduled my activities and events. I wasn't too surprised when I realized that though I was committed to my new sense of purpose and direction, many of our parents and students still longed for the good old days of the "once a month club." It took nearly a year for these parents to see the value of this new approach, but they eventually became key players in the work.

This reminds me of the late Dave Busby who shared in a personal interview the "keys to an effective youth ministry" with a group of young and very inexperienced youth pastors. I will never forget him sharing his own experiences as a youth pastor and how he one day decided that "enough was enough." Knowing that a full calendar did not equate with real success, Busby gave a clear charge to his staff. His words were simple but profound. They would do nothing unless they had the time to bathe the activity or event in prayer. Slavery to the calendar ended, and real life began in his youth ministry as those things that deserved top billing actually received it!

When looking at effective planning for events that make an eternal difference, a number of things should be considered:

1. **Ask two key questions:** What is the purpose of this event? What will it accomplish long-term?

2. **Am I willing to clear my calendar in order to give the event or activity the time and energy needed to plan and adequately prepare?** Effective events are determined by effective planning, and effective planning takes time. I remember that Noah began to build the ark before it started to rain!

3. **Does this event fit with the goals and objectives of my church and my pastor?** All too often, youth pastors dream big dreams but fail to inform their pastors or their leadership teams. They find out too late that they are the only ones holding to that dream. This can unnecessarily bring about real disappointment and disillusionment.

4. **Do we have a team of people ready to make this event happen?** Building a team is key to every area of youth ministry; this will either ensure success in carrying out the event or bring unbelievable frustration as you try to make it happen by yourself. Whether you have a staff team or a volunteer group of adult and student leaders, you must not try to be the "Lone Ranger" in this effort.

5. **Am I willing to share the vision for the event and then allow others to be involved?** A wise youth pastor understands that he is limited. He is limited by his abilities, his endurance, and his sphere of influence. Once he comes to that simple realization, he can begin to "give away" the vision. It is an amazing thing to see people catch the fever of a God-birthed dream! They can then accomplish much more with maximum effectiveness.

6. **What will it cost in terms of time, resources, space, and**

money? Frustration is the by-product of refusing to ask this question.

7. **Is this the right time?** Good ideas and good timing bring great results.

8. **Will I be able to see the event through to the end, or will I get bored and drift on to other things?** This sounds like a silly question, but it is not! Surely, if you are in charge of leading a "big event" you will see it through. I can tell you that many people are dreamers, but their thresholds for monotonous planning and preparation is low. They soon move on to bigger and better things, leaving others to see the event through.

9. **How will I know whether the event is successful?** What will be my standard of evaluation? Have I determined the purpose of this event and how it contributes to the overall strategy of the ministry? Who will I ask to be involved in the process of evaluating the event?

10. **How will I follow up on this event?** You know the feeling. It's late at night, the custodian is turning the lights off, and you are heading out of the building. A wave of satisfaction washes over you. The event was awesome! Tons of students came, they thought your event was cool, the parents were smiling, and the students even liked the T-shirt you gave out! By all standards, it was a huge success. Or was it? Is it possible that the result won't be known for some time, since follow-up is just as important as the event itself?

We have made the follow-up to any evangelistic event as much a priority as the event itself. When decisions are made, thorough counseling is always provided on a one-on-one basis. Immediately following the event, the student responding to Christ is contacted by a member of our follow-up team as well as by a member of our church staff. This is time-consuming but absolutely necessary.

Many students who come to our events have little

other contact with our church; therefore, it is imperative that we establish a relationship with them quickly. Our most successful method of follow-up has been to have the person who provided the counseling do the actual follow-up with the student. That way, there is an established relationship, which can be to built upon.

11. **Do I believe God is leading me to do this?** This is the bottom line and the one factor that will keep you moving forward even if things get difficult!

Over the past six months, a mentoring group I am involved with has been looking at the life of Nehemiah. This group is made up of fourteen sophomore and junior guys. As we have walked the roads of Nehemiah's life, from cupbearer to wall-builder to leader, we have been reminded of the questions listed above. His event was critical to the people of Israel. The city of Jerusalem was devastated, but he knew he could make a difference. More than that, he felt the call of God to go and rebuild the wall surrounding the city. Like Nehemiah, we have been challenged to keep an eternal perspective (the bigger picture) in how we live our life, and what we give our time to. And like Nehemiah, if we follow the principles of godly event planning, follow-through, and follow-up, we will see eternal fruit in the life of our ministry and in the lives of our students.

TAKE A RISK AND LIVE TO TELL ABOUT IT!

I love to read about people who are risk takers. Just a few weeks ago, George H.W. Bush, our forty-first president, took a flying leap out of an airplane! Celebrating his birthday, he took a risk and accomplished one of his life goals. Some people might scratch their heads and wonder if the White House years adversely affected his senses, but Bush enjoyed the rush and excitement of falling through the sky under the canopy of a parachute. Not bad for an 80-year-old man!

In the arena of ministry, there are those who are risk takers and those who are accustomed to maintenance. Neither is better than the other, and the church benefits from the work of both. But as you plan events that affect the life of your youth ministry, and ultimately your church, let me challenge you to be a risk taker. This doesn't mean that you recklessly make decisions that can endanger yourself or your church, but risk taking does allow you to achieve greater results than you normally might think possible. Risk takers see past the obvious and are willing to move out with an entrepreneurial spirit. They tend to see the possibilities more than the roadblocks. They don't ignore the speed bumps and warning signs ahead, but they don't let obstacles deter them either. But there is a potential downside in taking risks! Sometimes you take risks and things don't work out as you had hoped. That is always a possibility. But as the old saying goes, "nothing ventured, nothing gained!"

Second Baptist Church is a metropolitan church drawing people from all over the Houston area. Our church, led by our senior pastor, has a vision to reach the city for Christ. It is not a nice wish for us; it is a mandate we sense from God. Our passion as a church is to fulfill in practical ways the mandate found in Matthew 28:19–20. To do that, we are constantly looking for creative ways to present the gospel and give people the opportunity to respond to Christ. Risk taking is encouraged, and those who dream big dreams find an opportunity to work and serve.

Last year, our church decided to bring in Team Impact, a group of athletes who use feats of strength to gain the attention of their audience and then present the gospel in a clear and unapologetic way. Our high school ministry was asked to lead this event. Immediately, we began to sense the incredible opportunity before us. Though an event like this had never been done at Second Baptist, and it seemed a little odd compared with other evangelistic efforts we had been involved in, we saw momentum build in anticipation of the week. In staff meetings prior to the Team Impact Crusade, there was recognition of the risk involved in making this a city-wide event. What if no one came? What if we spent all this money, and no one came to faith in Christ? What if people looked at this kind of event and wondered what were we thinking? What if the only people who thought this was a good idea were body builders, NASCAR fans, and people with a passion for breaking bricks? The pressure of the risk we were taking was a present reality throughout the months leading up to the event.

When the crusade finally arrived, we were ready. Preparation had gone well, and many people had joined the leadership team and were taking ownership of the vision behind the event. I sensed a real and growing anticipation among our church family, and many were committed to bringing their friends and neighbors to the crusade. When the week was over, we were simply amazed! The Team Impact men had spoken in 131 public and private school assemblies, appeared on radio and television programs promoting the event, attended fourteen high school football games meeting students and their parents, spoken to Sunday school classes throughout our church (encouraging the church family to bring their families and friends), and worked as hard as they possibly could in preparing for a God-honoring event!

Each day they spoke in school assemblies, and each night they performed and ministered to large crowds at both our Woodway and West Campus locations. When the crusade was over and we were able to evaluate the event, we were thrilled! Over one thousand first-time decisions for Christ were recorded, with 291 of them choosing to be baptized at the end of each night's service. Those one thousand decisions had come from all over the Houston area. Many had no church home and were looking for a place to serve and grow! We had initiated a strong and positive relationship with the local schools and opened up a door of friendship and dialogue with school administrators and principals. We were convinced that the time, energy, and money spent were well worth it!

As our staff met to discuss the crusade, we made a simple "reminder list" to guide us in future event planning. The following is a partial list of those items:

1. **Communicate your vision clearly!** We knew we had to sell the idea to our church family. They would "buy in" wholeheartedly if we did a good job sharing our vision.

2. **Work hard, and don't give up!** God doesn't "need" me to bring about a strong and powerful work in the lives of people. He can use the rocks and trees if He so chooses! But He does choose to use us, and His work through us is magnified as we work hard and "work smart"! Many days were spent knocking on the doors of school administrators and principals. Many were not interested, but we did not give up. In our minds, the "cause for the Kingdom" was worth the effort!

3. **Involve a cross section of people from the church family to make the event happen!** Singles were in charge of the staging, materials, and meals for the athletes each day. Senior adults were responsible for shuttling the athletes from school to school for ten days. Children were challenged to bring their parents and friends from their neighborhood, and students were instrumental in the various methods of promotion. Our married adults made up a significant part of the six hundred fifty counselors we needed each night. The result was that this event became a church-wide project that all ages and areas could support.

4. **Think outside the box!** Our thought quickly became, *what else could we do to reach people through this event?* For three months, we asked ourselves that question and over and over came up with new and fresh ideas of promotion. Most of these ideas had nothing to do with money; they just required fresh thinking and a willingness to be creative! For example, a local cleaner attached a promotional flyer to every garment given back to patrons. Several fast-food chains flooded our area with promotional cards attached to filled orders, and a number of our students used their cars as "moving billboards," encouraging people to attend the crusade!

5. **Communicate like crazy!** This is always the hardest and most frustrating part of any event. Just when we thought everybody was on board with us, someone would ask us, "Is that brick smashing thing still on?" E-mail quickly became our best friend, and we burned up the line with information about the event and how our church family could reach people for Christ. It became our highest priority to make sure that the staff was on the same page, and when we found "holes" in our plan; we worked quickly to fix the problem.

6. **Do heart-checks periodically.** Our staff was fixated with this event for two months, and we wanted to be sure that our own relationship with Christ was fresh and growing. We would often gather our youth ministry staff together for times of prayer and accountability. Our focus was not on how the event was coming along; instead, it was on how we were doing in our own walks with God. We were keenly aware that events like this could easily warp our priorities and impair our motivation. We wanted to be sure that we did the right things, for the right reasons, using the right methods!

A FAIR WARNING TO ALL!

A significant danger in activities and events is that they can easily become the "end all" for your ministry. The youth ministry road is littered with youth pastors who sold out to events and ended up out of business! Events by themselves are simply calendar hogs that demand more and more time and energy. If you build your ministry primarily on activities and events, even if they are good and purposeful, you will become disillusioned and discouraged. You will find yourself in a constant race to do "bigger and better" and will find it impossible to keep up. Worse, you will find yourself questioning the call of God upon your life and your own passion for youth ministry. Such is the danger of over-emphasizing events and activities. Through twenty-five years of working with students, I have been reminded repeatedly that the key is to center the ministry on a Christ-honoring philosophy and purpose, and then allow the activities and events to give support to that purpose. If we choose to "do the usual unusually well," we will find ministry to be an exciting place indeed. It's what we do the rest of the year in developing student disciples, working with adult leaders and parents, and building a consistent and mature ministry, that gives opportunities for big events to have a place of meaning and purpose in our work!

GOD...AND GUITARS

Tom Phillips

I had a front row seat when the worship leader said to the five hundred or so students in the room, "OK, everybody, stand up and let's worship." The band started up—loud and strong—and the leader began to sing, "You are the Lord, the famous one." I glanced around the room at the different students present. Many were looking at the words and singing enthusiastically. Some had their eyes closed, very obviously focusing on the words and on the worship. Some were goofing around. Some were half-heartedly singing. Some were looking down, with no expression on their face.

As I stood there looking around, I had many questions running through my mind.

- What is "worship"?
- How do I teach worship to my students?
- How does worship affect our student meetings?

In this chapter, we will explore these questions together and discover what the Word of God says to us about worship.

WHAT IS WORSHIP?

The idea of worship appears more than 250 times in the Bible: approximately 175 times in the Old Testament and 80 times in the New Testament.[1] Our English word *worship* means "worth-ship." The word "worship," in its simplest form, is simply "humbling ourselves before a Holy God." It means "to bow down, or to do homage." John 4:24 says, "God is Spirit, and those who worship Him must worship in spirit and truth."

When we worship God, we are honoring Him. Like the angels, we are saying, "You are worthy, O Lord, to receive glory and honor and power" (Revelation 4:11).

Read how various authors have defined "worship":

Tony Beckett, in his book, *Real Life, Real Worship,* says: "Worship may be regarded as the direct acknowledgement to God of His nature, attributes, ways and claims, whether by the outgoing of the heart in praise and thanksgiving or by deeds done in such acknowledgement."[2]

Warren Wiersbe says this about worship:

> Worship is the believer's response of all that they are—mind, emotions, will and body—to what God is and says and does. This response has its mystical side in subjective experience and its practical side in objective obedience to God's revealed will. Worship is a loving response that is balanced by the fear of the Lord and it is a deepening response as the believer comes to know God better.[3]

A.W. Tozer says that worship is "the most sacred offering of ourselves and our worship to the God and Father of our Lord Jesus Christ."[4]

Rick Warren says that worship is simply "bringing pleasure to God."[5]

Two things at work in worship:

Worship involves attitude.

It is an attitude of humility, of reverence, of bowing before a Holy God. We see the example of this in Isaiah 6 where Isaiah saw the Lord and said, "Woe is me, for I am undone! Because I am a man of unclean lips, and I dwell in the midst of a people of unclean lips; for my eyes have seen the King, the LORD of hosts" (Isaiah 6:5).

Worship involves action.

In Matthew 4:10, Jesus quotes God's words to Moses when He tells Satan, "You shall worship the LORD your God, and Him only you shall serve." The word "worship" in that verse has the idea of service.

HOW DO WE, AS STUDENT LEADERS, TEACH WORSHIP TO OUR STUDENTS?

It is important to teach worship in such a way that we move our students to a greater awareness of God, His work in their lives, and their responses to Him.

Let's examine four steps to worship in a student group.

1. Worship depends on a personal relationship with God.

Before we can teach a student to worship, we need to teach him how to have a personal relationship with God. How many times have unsaved people come to your church meeting and felt completely out of place in your worship—because they didn't know the person you were worshiping? The gospel must be presented simply and clearly on a regular basis with opportunity for students to begin a new relationship with Christ.

A perfect example of this principle at work is in John 4, where Jesus meets the Samaritan woman at the well. Jesus' goal was to turn this woman into a true worshiper. Jesus knew that His Father was seeking that kind of worshiper. Jesus proceeded to establish a dialogue with her about the deepest need in her soul—a living hope. The conversation progressed to the subject of worship, and Jesus broke down her preconceived ideas of worship. Then He proceeded to let her know that she could worship the true God "in spirit and in truth."

Once that relationship has begun, we are charged to help that relationship become dynamic. If the relationship is cultivated to the point of being genuine and fruitful, your students will be taking the first steps toward understanding the nature and character of the God they have accepted.

2. *Worship develops from your reverence for God.*

The more your students know about who God is, the more they will understand how to show reverence for Him. The more your students reverence God, the more they will long to worship Him.

You need to teach your young people who God is and what God is like. These are some of His attributes to review with your teens:

> God is personal.—John 3:16
> God is eternal.—Psalm 90:2
> God is Spirit.—John 4:24
> God is all-powerful.—Matt. 19:26
> God is everywhere.—Psalm 139:7, 8
> God is sovereign.—Daniel 4:35
> God is unchanging.—James 1:17
> God is good.—Psalm 34:8
> God is righteous and just.—Psalm 7:9-12
> God is holy.—Isaiah 6:35

These attributes are not just a résumé on God; they make a definitive difference in the everyday life of a student. As you teach these attributes, the students have to be able to make a personal connection. Your students' mental pictures of worship will emanate from their mental pictures of God. Students should learn about God from all we do—from our music, our activities, our discipleship, our messages, and even from our announcements.

3. *Worship is defined by your response to God.*

We need to teach students that our worship of God goes beyond thoughts and words—it manifests itself through our lives by our service to God. In Romans 12:1–2 we read that the reasonable response in worship is to "present your body a living sacrifice, holy, acceptable to God." In other words, it is more than the songs we sing. It is more than the prayers we pray.

It is more than the emotion that accompanies those things. Worship is also responding to God in commitment. The culmination of worship in a student's life should be when the student takes his or her life and puts it in God's hands for His use exclusively. That's the challenge of worship in youth work—to bring students to that point.

I have seen this work numerous times in the lives of students at Word of Life camp. Everything we do all week looks forward to the dedication service. Our songs make God big, our testimonies make God personal, our Bible hours make God alive, and our activities make God visible. So at the end of the week when we give the campers an opportunity to respond to God by placing their lives in His hands, their pictures of God motivate their response.

So fresh in my memory is one particular night when I personally observed this. My son was in Israel with a summer short-term missions team from Word of Life. All excited, he called me and exclaimed, "Dad, did you know that Jesus is coming back?" I assured him that I had heard that a time or two and that I believed it with all my heart, but my son just kept saying, "If Jesus is coming back anytime, it could be soon, and I need to serve Him with my life." His life has never been the same since that call. That's it! That's what we are looking for in student work. We are looking for our students to come to a point in worship where they reach up to God and out to others.

4. Worship is displayed in our daily routines.

Warren Wiersbe says: "Worship ought to be the constant attitude and activity of the dedicated believer. What we've been doing privately all week we do publicly as we come together with the people of God on the Lord's Day."[6]

Colossians 3:23 says that everything we do should be done enthusiastically—for God and not for men. When we live in constant devotion and reverence to God, we do all that we do to please Him. That is the simplest yet the ultimate form of worship—taking each breath, speaking each word, doing each duty, completing each assignment for Him.

I was the camp speaker at Hartland Christian Camp in Central California. I was walking down by the lake preparing myself for the chapel service when a boy ran up to me. I have forgotten his name—but his face is indelibly etched in my mind. In fact, I can still smell his breath as he grabbed my arm and got right up in my face. He said, "What would you do to me if I threw you in the lake?"

I didn't have time for this. I was getting ready to present the Word to 250 needy students, and this kid was about to ruin my night. I pushed him away and said, "Just leave me alone, you little punk." I said it in my gruff voice, to make sure he understood. He just looked at me with a confused, almost dazed look and walked away. I discovered that night that if my worship was wrong in my daily routine, it influenced my ministry—particularly in this youth meeting. I couldn't get up and speak until I had made things right with that young man.

HOW DOES WORSHIP AFFECT YOUR STUDENT MEETING?

1. *Your worship should affect your preaching and teaching.*

When a student leader prepares a message, he should ask God to stir his own heart with the message first. Before the throne of God, he should ask the Spirit of God to bring him face to face with the Living God. Then, standing before the students, the challenge of bringing them face to face with God will be an extension of his own personal contact.

This becomes an act of worship on your part. If your preaching is an act of worship, it will be evidenced in practical ways:

The Word of God will come alive to the students.

You will have such passion that they can't help but see it.

The Word of God will motivate to action.

Your students will have a desire to obey the Word that they hear. James 1:22 says, "But be ye doers of the word and not hearers only, deceiving yourselves." If your students are not motivated to action by the Word of God, there is something wrong with the delivery. The goal of every Bible study should be to make the Word of God "come alive."

The Word of God will change lives.

Your students will want to change from the inside out when your preaching is an act of worship. One speaker said, "My purpose statement in preaching is that every time I stand up and communicate the Word of God I want to see lives changed for eternity."

2. Your worship should affect your program.

Your music:

In his book, *Real Worship,* Warren Wiersbe says that there are five ways to evaluate your music:

1. *Does it have biblical content?*

    Does the music you hear in your student meetings reflect the doctrine you teach in your meeting? Does it reflect biblical truth?

2. *Does it have technical excellence?*

    Remember, everything you do is either acceptable or unacceptable to God—so do it right. Find the best musicians you can so that you can do it to the glory of God. I have become critically aware of the fact that everything we do teaches. Are we teaching excellence, or are we teaching mediocrity through our music?

3. *Are the musicians doing it for the right motive?*

    You might ask it this way: do they realize that God is the audience? After you select your musicians, get with them and make sure they are performing only for God. Think about it! A musician is a minister. What does the

Bible say about ministers? What are the qualifications for ministering the Word of God to others? Maybe you should do another tour through the Pastoral Epistles and review the qualifications for leadership in the church. I know that these are just students who love God and want to serve, but what is the life message they communicate daily? As you instruct the musicians, teach them to pray for power, passion, and purity in their delivery.

4. *Is it authentic?*

   Can the students in the audience see the Lord in the lives of those ministering? Do their faces communicate outwardly what is happening inwardly?

5. *Is it balanced?*

   Do you think Jesus was a radical or a conservative? Neither one—he was the perfect balance. For that reason, it is always best to seek a balance that pleases God. Ask the Lord to guide you to where the lines should be and stay within them.[7]

Your fellowship:

Your fellowship time should be encouraging, inclusive, and loving. Realizing that everything we do is either an acceptable or a putrid sacrifice to God is a sobering thought. It will motivate us to think through what we do before we minister to our students.

Warren Wiersbe says about your program, "Every ministry of the church should be a byproduct of worship. Ministry that's divorced from worship has no roots and therefore can produce no lasting fruits."[8]

3. Your view of worship should affect your planning!

If every ministry of the church is a byproduct of worship, how can we plan our individual gatherings so they are permeated with this goal? Perhaps we should ask ourselves, whose agenda is it anyway? Is your meeting on God's agenda or your agenda? As you plan your agenda, think about each aspect of the meeting. Everything that goes on in a meeting is a sacrifice to God. It is either an acceptable sacrifice to God or an unacceptable sacrifice to Him. Go through each aspect of your program and evaluate it by biblical criteria. Determine if it is acceptable or unacceptable to Him. So how can you tell?

Psalm 95 gives us a great gauge of whether our program is glorifying God or not.

- Does it bring out some aspect of God's character (Psalm 95:1–5)?
- Does it bring honor and glory to Him (Psalm 95:6)?
- Does it motivate your students to serve Him better (Psalm 95:7)?

PLANNING EACH PROGRAM WITH WORSHIP IN MIND

When you get ready to "build" a meeting, you start with the focus of the meeting.

Generally, that is the infusion of the Word. Since that is the focal point of the meeting, you should work backward and forward from that point.

1. What has God stirred up in your heart that you will share in the meeting?
2. Can you boil it down to one big idea?
3. Can you make that idea come alive in your teaching?
4. How can you garnish that idea with songs, dramas, testimonies, or group dynamics?
5. How can you season that idea with illustrations and applications?
6. How can you motivate your students to take that idea and use it as an agent of change in their lives to better please God?

Everything you do should flow to and from the focus of your meeting. That focus is the climax of a night of bringing praise and glory to God. When you build your meeting this way, it has focus and purpose.

YOUR VIEW OF WORSHIP SHOULD AFFECT YOUR DISCIPLESHIP

What is your definition of discipleship? Whatever it is, it should always include the aim of bringing students to the point of glorifying God. To be effective in that aim, your students need to grow in their knowledge of God. Therefore, in discipleship we need to help our students feel accountable to God, expressive to God, submissive to God, indebted to God, and ultimately motivated to serve God.

I was only fifteen when my youth leader told me that I needed to fall in love with God.

I was overwhelmed by his assignment, but for the next two years he took on the challenge of helping this teenage "goof-off" realize that spending my life on anything else but honoring God would be wasting my life. Praise the Lord that he didn't give up on me.

Along the way, one of the things he taught me was that service and worship are synonymous. My devotional life with God and my public service to God are inseparable. The use of my time and the performance of my ministry are all part of one focus: glorifying God in all.

What about your student ministry? Have you come to the place where you are focused on God's agenda, or are you experimenting with one trendy idea followed by another? Are you ready to say to God, "It's Your program, it's Your agenda, and my life is totally Yours, Lord"? Will you surrender your will to the one goal of being a sweet-smelling offering to Him?

Right about now you are saying, "OK, if you are so smart then tell me how to express worship and model worship. And please communicate with me how to teach the concept of worship to my students."

THE DAY WORSHIP BECAME REAL TO ME

I had been in full-time ministry for over twenty years without a real perception of what worship was all about—until the summer of 1999. I was judging student choirs in a national youth talent competition when I heard a song that grabbed me and changed my heart. As I listened to that song, the message of the song, coupled with the moving of the Holy Spirit of God, changed my motivation for ministry.

The words of the song were simple, but in an instant they captured what I had been trying to live out for the last twenty years. As I listened to the song, conviction, encouragement, and inspiration flooded my soul. I asked for a copy and read it over and over again—and as I read it, the Holy Spirit brought many Scripture references to my mind. I found a quiet place and sang the song to God as tears flooded my eyes. That's the day I realized how consuming worship can be in the life of God's children.

SCRIPTURE MEMORY SUGGESTIONS:

John 4:23–24
Isaiah 6:1–5
Luke 4:8
Romans 12:1–2
Psalm 115:1–8

SUGGESTED READING

Beckett, Tony. *Real Life, Real Worship.* Lincoln, NE: Back to the Bible Publishing, 2001.

Tozer, A.W. *Whatever Happened to Worship?* Camp Hill, PA: Christian Publications, 1985.

Wiersbe, Warren. *Real Worship.* Grand Rapids, MI: Baker Books, 2002.

NOTES

1. Tony Beckett, *Real Life, Real Worship* (Lincoln, NE: Back to the Bible Publishers, 2001).

2. Ibid.

3. Warren Wiersbe, *Real Worship* (Grand Rapids, MI: Baker Books, 2002), p. 95.

4. A.W. Tozer, *Whatever Happened to Worship?* (Camp Hill, PA: Christian Publications, 1985), p. 9.

5. Rick Warren, *The Purpose Driven Life* (Grand Rapids: Zondervan, 2002).

6. Wiersbe.

7. Ibid.

8. Ibid.

TEACHING ON PURPOSE WITH A PURPOSE

Mel Walker

Visualize the name and face of one of the junior high students in your church youth group. In fact, try to select a seventh grader, girl or guy—it's up to you. Now picture that same student six short years from now as they graduate from high school. That kid you are thinking about will walk across the stage and accept his or her diploma. You'll be there in the crowd of spectators and well-wishers proudly cheering him or her on to greater things. This particular student has gone through the entire scope of your youth ministry. From the Sunday school classes to the all-nighters; from camp to van trips; from banquets to amusement parks; and from missions trips to youth group meetings. As you sit there in the bleachers, will you have the confidence that this student is ready to face the world of college or maybe the work force? Will his or her experience in your church's youth ministry be one that prepared that person for life?

That six-year transition from seventh grader to high school graduate is where I believe youth ministry best accomplishes the purpose of the church. You get them as children (ever work with seventh grade boys?), and they leave you as young adults, demonstrated by that rite of passage called high school graduation. That six-year window, from seventh grade to high school graduation, gives youth workers a unique learning and growing environment for students. Everything we plan to do and everything we want to do as youth workers must happen during that six-year time frame. Everything! That's why I say that youth ministry best accomplishes the church's purpose during these critical years.

We have to fit everything we do into this incredibly short period. Most youth ministries are not responsible for the children's ministry (although we certainly should be strategically involved in their lives then), and most youth ministries are not accountable for adult ministries (although we should care enough to track our students throughout their adult lives.) However, we are responsible for them during their teenage years. The role of youth ministry is to teach, guide, mentor, disciple, train, motivate, exhort, and educate students as they move from childhood, through youth ministry, and then out into an adult world.

We must be willing to ask ourselves every single time one of our students graduates from high school and leaves our ministry, "Are they ready?" "Have I taught them everything they need for spiritual maturity?" These sobering questions express the reasons why your students need a comprehensive and intentional learning plan. Effective youth ministry mandates an exit strategy so to speak.

Let's start at the beginning. Keep that seventh grader in mind; now think about him or her from this perspective. When he graduates from high school six years from now, what do you want him to know? What biblical truth should she have learned? What doctrinal beliefs should she hold? What convictions or biblical principles should govern his life? What life skills should she possess? And what biblical values should she be able to apply to her life?

You have this six-year opportunity to invest in their lives. The lessons they need to learn may come during Sunday school, youth group time, small group interaction, or from some other educational setting. The instruction they need may also come from informal time spent with students before or after youth meetings and activities, wilderness trips, camping, or weekend retreats.

The point is, youth workers have been given the stewardship over the lives of teenagers for six years. Six short years. You get them as children—they leave you as young adults. What you teach them is very, very important. Your role is to prepare them spiritually for adulthood.

They'll leave the cozy confines of your church's youth ministry very, very soon to head off into an adult world where they'll likely be confronted about what they believe. They need to be prepared. They need to know what they believe and why; and they need to know how to back up those beliefs with Scripture. They also need a working knowledge of God's Word that will help them resist sin and temptation, and they need the tools to know how to "rightly divide the word of truth" on their own. Without an intentional learning plan, this is an impossible assignment.

I understand biblically that parents have the primary responsibility for the tasks mentioned above. Deuteronomy 6 and other passages place that burden directly on the shoulders of parents. Let's not take this truth lightly. However, one only needs to examine the Pastoral Epistles to understand that an effective and biblically based pastoral ministry must include "feeding the flock" and teaching God's people the life-changing truth of His Word.

That brings us back to the importance of developing an intentional and comprehensive learning plan for your ministry to junior high and senior high students. A few months ago, I attended what was advertised as the "largest youth workers' conference ever." Because of my interest in teaching and curriculum, I sat in on a workshop on writing lessons for teenagers. Early in the hour, the workshop presenter asked the two hundred or so attendees how many of them did not have their teaching lesson ready for the next Sunday or Wednesday. The overwhelming majority of youth workers attending raised their hands to indicate that indeed they were not prepared for their next teaching time.

This illustration exposes one of the basic weaknesses of modern-day youth ministry. There are too many youth pastors and youth workers who are not taking the time or initiative to develop a comprehensive, intentional learning plan for their students. It appears there are many who do not prepare much ahead of time for their next teaching responsibility.

To put a positive spin on this phenomenon, I am convinced that today's youth workers have the desire to be relevant at all costs. Now that doesn't sound so bad, except they may be sacrificing a comprehensive learning plan for their students in some misguided attempt to be relevant and current. The truth is many youth workers today are not equipped or disciplined to work out a six-year schedule for teaching their teenagers. I know that this sounds somewhat cynical. That is not my intention. I simply want youth workers to raise the bar on their teaching ministries. I want them to see the need to teach their students the "whole counsel of God" and the importance of the educational aspect of Christ's Great Commission when he instructed His followers to teach "them to observe all things that I have commanded you" (Matthew 28:20).

BIBLICAL PRINCIPLES OF EDUCATION

The Scriptures are filled with references illustrating the importance of a total plan of study as a major prerequisite for growth to spiritual maturity. Look at the educational principles in the passages listed below.

It is my own contention that every youth worker must develop a set curriculum—a comprehensive teaching plan for the educational ministries of the youth ministry. By making that statement, I am not saying that youth workers should necessarily look to some para-church organization or Christian publisher for their printed curricula; although in many cases this might be the best idea. (More about the advantages and disadvantages of using published curricula or writing your own curriculum will be presented later in this chapter.) I wonder about the validity of so many youth workers who claim to have the ability to write and produce their own curriculum and teaching

Scripture Passage	Educational Principle That Applies to Youth Ministry
Psalm 119:105—Your word is a lamp to my feet and a light to my path.	✓ We must show students that God's Word gives specific direction to their lives.
Matthew 28:19–20—Go therefore and make disciples of all the nations, baptizing them in the name of the Father and of the Son and of the Holy Spirit, teaching them to observe all things that I have commanded you; and lo, I am with you always, even to the end of the age. Amen.	✓ A key aspect of the Great Commission is that we teach everything Christ "commanded."
Acts 20:27— For I have not shunned to declare to you the whole counsel of God.	✓ We must remember to teach our students the "all" of God's Word.
Ephesians 4:11–16—And He Himself gave some to be apostles, some prophets, some evangelists, and some pastors and teachers, for the equipping of the saints for the work of ministry, for the edifying of the body of Christ, till we all come to the unity of the faith and of the knowledge of the Son of God, to a perfect man, to the measure of the stature of the fullness of Christ; that we should no longer be children, tossed to and fro and carried about with every wind of doctrine, by the trickery of men, in the cunning craftiness of deceitful plotting, but, speaking the truth in love, may grow up in all things into Him who is the head—Christ—from whom the whole body, joined and knit together by what every joint supplies, according to the effective working by which every part does its share, causes growth of the body for the edifying of itself in love.	✓ Specific educational elements are involved in God's grand purpose for His church. The key thing is that our objective is the spiritual maturity of our students.
1 Timothy 2:3–4—For this is good and acceptable in the sight of God our Savior, who desires all men to be saved and to come to the knowledge of the truth.	✓ The key ingredient of our ministries must be the salvation of our students.
2 Timothy 2:15—Be diligent to present yourself approved to God, a worker who does not need to be ashamed, rightly dividing the word of truth.	✓ We must teach our students the ability to study God's Word on their own so that they can "rightly" divide the "word of truth."
2 Timothy 3:10–17—But you have carefully followed my doctrine, manner of life, purpose, faith, longsuffering, love, perseverance, persecutions, afflictions, which happened to me at Antioch, at Iconium, at Lystra—what persecutions I endured. And out of them all the Lord delivered me. Yes, and all who desire to live godly in Christ Jesus will suffer persecution. But evil men and impostors will grow worse and worse, deceiving and being deceived. But you must continue in the things which you have learned and been assured of, knowing from whom you have learned them, and that from childhood you have known the Holy Scriptures, which are able to make you wise for salvation through faith which is in Christ Jesus. All Scripture is given by inspiration of God, and is profitable for doctrine, for reproof, for correction, for instruction in righteousness, that the man of God may be complete, thoroughly equipped for every good work.	✓ Teaching the Word of God is essential for spiritual growth.

materials. Certainly some youth workers have the ability to develop an intentional and comprehensive learning plan that includes creative and well-designed individual lessons for their teenagers. However, my experience with youth workers has revealed that the majority of youth workers should instead look for other sources of materials and curricula.

Shepherds have the responsibility to feed their sheep. That includes the development of a "balanced diet," where youth workers conscientiously take the initiative to plan a total learning plan of everything students need to know before they exit your ministries. If we want our students to grow into spiritual maturity as they progress through our youth ministries, we should equip them through our teaching ministry. (See 2 Timothy 3:16–17.) Once that comprehensive teaching plan is in place, youth workers can look to a variety of sources for specific materials and lessons that fit their purpose and educational plan.

INGREDIENTS OF A COMPREHENSIVE LEARNING PLAN

A curriculum is a set of courses or subjects that when taken together form the basis of what the student needs to finish his or her desired program. For example, high schools, colleges, and universities all boast of set curricula that give the student everything needed to graduate from that particular institution or program. Likewise, a youth ministry curriculum gives students everything they need for spiritual maturity before they exit from your ministry as a graduating high school senior.

I have not attempted to provide an exhaustive list of everything that should be included in an intentional comprehensive learning plan for youth ministry, but I have listed the basic ingredients of what should be included as students progress from seventh graders to graduating seniors. These basic points are listed here in the form of questions to help youth workers evaluate their own progress in this strategic aspect of ministry.

1. Does each student know Jesus Christ as his or her personal Savior, and is each student growing in Him? In other words, how do you know that each student is born again and growing in a relationship with Christ? Practically speaking, you must present the gospel message often throughout your ministry and have several opportunities for yourself or other adult youth workers to talk to all of your students individually about their assurance of salvation.

2. Does each student have a basic knowledge of Scripture— including the ability to interpret the Bible grammatically, historically, and literally? Second Timothy 2:15 uses the phrase "rightly dividing the word of truth," and that is the basic idea here. We want our students to understand fundamental Bible knowledge such as the books of the Bible, how to study the Bible for themselves (including a personal, daily devotional life), and God's overall plan for mankind.

3. Does each student have a basic grasp of Bible doctrine, and do they know what they believe? It is not our intent necessarily that our students turn out to be master theologians like Calvin or Luther, but we do want them to know what they believe and why. They may be confronted about their faith as they go through high school, but that is even more likely to happen when they go off to college or into the work force. Apologetics, or the ability to defend what one believes, is something that is very attractive to today's students. Make sure that your students know what they believe, and train them to defend their beliefs when confronted.

4. Are your students actively seeking and following God's will for their lives? Each youth worker, I'm sure, is very concerned about the students knowing and doing the will of God in their lives. That's why it is so important to intentionally and systematically schedule time in your teaching to present biblical truth concerning this important subject. Not only do we want our students to consider what God wants them to do in various life decisions (like where to go to college, whom to marry, or what career path to take), but it is also imperative that some of your students prayerfully consider that God may be calling them into full-time, vocational ministry. God is still in the business of calling certain people into career ministry. (See Acts 13:2.) It has been my experience that many teens would not actively seek God's will for their lives unless they were instructed to do so from a biblical lesson or series of lessons on the subject.

5. Does each student have the ability to answer the tough questions and face the key issues of life from a biblical perspective? All of today's students are going to have to answer some of life's tough questions as they mature into an adult world of sin, temptation, lust, greed, and materialism. It is especially important that they know where to turn for answers. They are also going to face many key issues or questionable matters as they grow up and move out on their own. Let's face it: their world is going to be quite a bit different from the world their parents knew. When I was growing up, for example, my parents had no idea that the world would soon be encircled by the Internet with its new and varied forms of temptation. By the way, when my wife and I were raising our children, we had no idea that our daughter would grow up and move to Europe. The questions and issues of life change as culture changes. It is critically important that youth workers teach students to go to the Word of God for answers. They must learn how to be discerning, to think critically and biblically, to find in the Scriptures the real answers for life's toughest questions and most challenging issues. (For example, what matters about thought-life, dating and relationships, sex and moral purity, friends, music, money and materialism, violence and war, suicide, abortion, and other moral issues? The list goes on and on.)

6. Does each student know how to make Bible-based personal convictions? In response to these kinds of questions and issues, we also want our students to have the ability and confidence to make personal and biblical convictions. We want our students to have the courage to stand up for what is right and to not do what is wrong (as Daniel did in Daniel 1:8, or as Shadrach, Meshach, and Abed-Nego did in Daniel 3:17–18).

7. *Is each student personally involved in serving the Lord in and through the local church?* Youth workers must teach their students to make the local church a priority—including such important lifestyle values as serving and tithing. We are doing our students a long-term disservice if we fail to emphasize the importance of involvement in and commitment to the local church. We must motivate students to get involved in church, and we must give them significant opportunities to be actively involved.

8. *Does each student have a positive and growing relationship with his or her parents?* There are other important topics, of course, that could be included in a comprehensive teaching plan for teenagers. However, I would be remiss to exclude an emphasis on teens' relationships to their parents and families. It is my conviction that youth pastors should make this topic a priority in their teaching ministries for a couple of very important reasons. First of all, today's students desperately need a positive relationship with their parents. Second, focusing on the positive role of parents in the lives of their teenagers will help you gain parental support of the overall youth ministry.

SETTING EDUCATIONAL OBJECTIVES FOR YOUTH MINISTRY

There are three important objectives to keep in mind when planning a total learning plan for students as they progress and mature through their teenage years in your church's youth ministry.

1. What do you want your students to **know**?
2. What do you want your students to **do**?
3. What do you want your students to **be**?

Youth workers must keep an "exit strategy" in mind for the students who are coming through our youth ministries. Remember our opening illustration about your junior high student who will graduate from your ministry six short years from now? These three overarching objectives will help guide our selection of teaching topics for our own curriculum. Our curriculum is the overall set of topics we present to our students as they progress through our youth ministry.

For instance, if we want our students to know Jesus Christ as their personal Savior, then we will clearly present the gospel message. If we want them to have a basic knowledge of Scripture, we will teach them the grand scope of the Bible. If we want them to have a basic understanding of Bible doctrine, we will clearly and systematically teach those things to them. If we want our students to share Christ with others and to form their own biblical convictions, we will train our students to do those things. Finally, if we want our students to be long-term and fruitful church members as adults, we will make sure that our youth ministries highlight those life goals.

See how it works? Our youth ministry curricula are the comprehensive learning plans that we have intentionally developed to give our students everything they need for spiritual maturity before they leave our ministries.

A final key aspect of an intentional learning plan for our youth ministries is the importance of having a fundamental knowledge of age-group characteristics when developing or selecting the topics to teach to students. Most youth workers appreciate what used to be called "human growth and development"—the fact that, for example, a seventh-grade boy is vastly different from a twelfth-grade girl. I encourage all youth workers to think carefully through the topics that should or should not be presented to junior high students and the methods of teaching that might or might not be appropriate to use with particular age groups.

WRITING YOUR OWN TEACHING MATERIALS

This leaves us with one final question concerning this issue: should youth workers design their own curricula or even write their own materials or individual lessons? I have talked with scores of youth workers who are doing just that. The trend in youth ministry today is an eclectic approach toward teaching. Many youth workers tend to teach random or miscellaneous topics that are selected based upon the interests of the students (I know of several churches that survey their teens in order to determine what topics the students want to hear about), current events, or other arbitrary factors. While I would surely endorse a certain amount of flexibility in the selection of subjects to teach the students, I firmly believe that a well-planned, holistic, and comprehensive curriculum (teaching teenagers everything they need for spiritual maturity as they move from seventh grade into adulthood) is essential for effective youth ministry.

ADVANTAGES TO USING PUBLISHED MATERIALS

There are some basic yet important advantages in adopting a set curriculum from an established Christian education publisher. One of the most important reasons, but probably one that is not readily recognized, is that you can identify the doctrinal position of the materials based on who published them. Likewise, if you randomly select teaching materials from a variety of publishers or from non-denominational publishers, you must work harder to recognize the doctrinal position that is presented in the lessons.

Earlier in this chapter, I wrote about my experience attending the huge conference with thousands of other youth workers. The conference's display area was filled with about five hundred exhibitors who were hawking everything from wilderness camping trips to fund-raising candy supplies. My curiosity drew me to one exhibit with a huge sign, "Bible Curriculum." Their book racks were filled with teachers' guides on several individual books of the Bible. I reached for that company's materials on the New Testament Book of 1 Corinthians because I wanted to see their position on sign-gifts and the charismatic movement. To my chagrin, this teacher's book did not even mention speaking in tongues or other sign-gifts. Obviously, this publishing company didn't take a stand on that topic because they wanted to sell youth materials to both charismatic and non-charismatic churches. My point here is this—youth workers must know the doctrinal position of the publisher before using those materials with their students.

Another advantage of utilizing a published curriculum is that it usually features a higher quality of production than an individual youth worker could do. Using published materials can save time for the youth worker because curriculum publishers often supply additional resources, background material, and other helps that the youth worker would otherwise have to locate on his own.

These materials often employ trained and experienced educational specialists who have the big picture concerning the needs and characteristics of today's teenagers. The writers and developers of these products can present a wider perspective of what is happening around the country and in other churches. Many local church youth workers do not have this larger scope because they are working in a single community with their own youth group.

DISADVANTAGES OF USING PUBLISHED MATERIALS

Of course, there are some inherent weaknesses in the selection and use of materials from outside publishers. If you have ever taught from published curricula you have undoubtedly had to adapt it and change it some to fit the needs of your students. By the way, I often tell youth workers that there are usually three ways to approach the use of published youth lessons. You may have to "tweak it" so that it fits the needs of your students; you may have to "trash it" because you know that particular topic, or lesson, or method of teaching won't work with your class; or you might just want to "try it" as is. Who knows? The writers and publishers may know what they are doing.

You may also have wondered about how current or relevant these products are for your specific youth group. And certainly, you will need to closely evaluate the doctrinal position of the publisher and writer. As I mentioned above, it is critically important that you put materials with solid Bible content in front of your students.

One other major disadvantage is that published materials require funds for the teaching supplies. Many publishers offer teacher manuals, some kind of visual aids, and student handouts or books, as well as a wide variety of other educational resources. Each church will need to evaluate its budget to see if the use of materials should be a financial priority. Some churches have decided not to invest in quality and professional teaching and learning materials for their students. Those churches should seriously and prayerfully think through the stewardship issues involved in making sure that students have high-quality and biblically based study materials in their hands.

ADVANTAGES OF WRITING AND DEVELOPING YOUR OWN MATERIALS OR LESSONS

Another attractive option is writing and producing new lessons and teaching materials. If you have the skills to do so, there are some real advantages to this. It makes the teacher or youth leader study on his own, and therefore the learning process is probably greater. It also helps develop the youth worker's own creativity since he has to put so much creative energy into studying the Scriptures, writing the lesson, planning the Bible learning activities or methods of teaching, and developing his own audiovisuals or other teaching materials. This process is also usually cheaper for the church. However, I have found that a youth worker who develops his own material must spend a certain amount of money for study, research, books, equipment, and other needs.

Probably the biggest advantage is how the youth worker can cater the curriculum to the needs of his own students. The published material may be able to offer the big picture of what most teenagers are like today, but the individual youth worker should know his own students. He knows their educational backgrounds, social perspectives, and cultural distinctives. He knows if his group is comprised of a majority of seniors or a majority of underclassmen. He knows the size of the group, and he knows what the specific teaching environment (or classroom) is like. All of these things are huge advantages in the development of Bible lessons that may or may not fit a particular church or youth group.

DISADVANTAGES OF WRITING & DEVELOPING YOUR OWN MATERIALS OR LESSONS

I often caution youth workers who tell me that they want to develop their own materials that there are some real drawbacks to that idea. First, the development of quality materials and lessons takes a great amount of study, preparation, and lesson organization. Each youth worker will need to ask himself if he really has that much time to dedicate to this discipline. Also, writing his own lessons takes a specific set of writing, communication, organizational, and even design skills. To be very blunt here: I know tons of youth pastors who have excellent relational skills, but I have met only a few youth workers who have the communication and organizational skills to produce quality educational materials.

There is one other major caution here. Some youth workers are excellent communicators who have real abilities to teach

God's Word to teenagers. I know many, many youth workers who have very good up-front skills and who definitely have the passion and ability to teach teenagers. However, what happens in their absence, while they are writing their own lessons? Could someone teach from the notes with the same zeal and interest as the person who developed the outline? I encourage all teachers to keep this question in mind as they prepare to teach. Who could teach for you if you couldn't be there? From time to time, a substitute teacher doing his or her own lesson may be appropriate and even necessary, but what about the comprehensive learning plan that the teenagers need?

ON A FINAL NOTE

Over fifteen years ago, well-known author Robert Fulghum wrote his best-selling book titled, *All I Really Need to Know I Learned in Kindergarten*. It contained such well-intentioned lessons as, "Share everything," "Don't hit people," and "Clean your own mess." With my apologies to Fulghum, I sincerely believe that all youth workers should teach: "All I really need to know I learned in church." The development of an intentional and comprehensive learning plan for students is essential for their growth toward spiritual maturity. We only have them for six short years. It's almost graduation time.

BIBLIOGRAPHY

Barna, George. *Transforming Children into Spiritual Champions.* Ventura, CA: Regal Books/Gospel Light, 2003.

Ford, LeRoy. *Design for Teaching & Training.* Eugene, OR: Wipf & Stock Publishers, 2002.

Fulghum, Robert. *All I Really Need to Know I Learned in Kindergarten.* New York: Ivy Books, 1986.

Gronlund, Norman E. *Writing Instructional Objective for Teaching and Assessment.* 7th ed. Upper Saddle River, NJ: Pearson/Merrill Prentice Hall, 2004.

Gregory, John Milton. *The Seven Laws of Teaching.* Rev. ed. Grand Rapids, MI: Baker Books, 1995.

LeFever, Marlene D. *Creative Teaching Methods.* Colorado Springs, CO: Cook Communications, 1996.

Richards, Lawrence O. *Creative Bible Teaching.* Chicago: Moody Press, 1977.

DID YOU HEAR WHAT I SAID?*

Lee Vukich and Steve Vandegriff

This chapter will show you the methods of teaching Christ used with His twelve disciples. Teaching may be in a Bible study, Sunday school class, Sunday evening, Wednesday night, or special event. How important is teaching to your ministry? The answer to that question is reflected in the attitude of Christ toward teaching as recorded in the gospels.

TEACHING METHODS OF CHRIST

When we talk about teaching, teaching methods, and the application of those methods, we must look to our Lord. Jesus is the prototype of teaching that we are to follow. He is the master-teacher. Many volumes have been written about the teaching styles of Christ. Libraries contain hundreds of books that examine and explain how Christ trained and communicated truth to His core followers and to the crowds. We will simply list methods that Christ incorporated in His teaching and then examine and explain how these methods pertain to students.

Jesus began His ministry as a teacher, and He remained one until His ascension. "Teacher" is one of the titles that Jesus was called most frequently while ministering on earth. As we examine any one of the gospels, we find that term applied to Him (e.g. Luke 6:40, 7:40, 8:49, 9:38, 10:25, 11:45, 12:13, 18:18,

*Taken from *Timeless Youth Ministry*, Moody Publishers, Copyright 2002 by Lee Vukich and Steve Vandergriff.

19:39, 20:21, 28, 39, 21:7, 22:11). Jesus said of Himself, "You call me Teacher and Lord, and you say well, for so I am" (John 13:13). The followers of Christ were called disciples or pupils, indicating that they were being instructed by a teacher. Jesus was the ultimate teacher. Even the prominent Jews who failed to recognize Him as Messiah quickly acknowledged His special abilities as a teacher (John 3:2, Mark 12:14).

Jesus is not referred to as a preacher in the gospel accounts, even though He did preach as well as teach: "And Jesus went about all Galilee, teaching in their synagogues, preaching the gospel of the kingdom" (Matthew 4:23). Four different words are utilized in the Gospels for the term "preaching." The word used in Luke 9:60 has the connotation, "to tell toughly," and is only used in the gospels. Other connotations include: "tell the good news," "cry or proclaim as a herald," and finally, "say" or "speak."

The teaching of Jesus was always full of life and the reality of life. He stood among the people and communicated in their environments and thoughts, tying them to spiritual truth. For example, what prompted the imagery used in Matthew 5:14 and John 3:8; 4:34–35; 6:35; 7:37–38; 8:12; 15:1–7? Pay attention to how He constantly uses common items to draw them into a new teaching or spiritual truth.

Jesus' most frequently used method is still viable when teaching teens. The teacher asks questions to make certain that he is understood fully by the listeners. The students then have the opportunity to ask questions and clarify the teaching. Obviously, uninterrupted discourse is easier, but is less valuable. Most of the material is readily forgotten as average teens cannot take it all in or carry it with them. Leaders are needed that will study this method of Christ and apply it into their ministry.

SPECIFIC EXAMPLES OF CHRIST'S TEACHINGS

The first example comes from John 2:23–25, which gives us information concerning Christ as a teacher, "Now when He was in Jerusalem at the Passover, during the feast, many believed in His name, when they saw the signs which He did. But Jesus did not commit Himself to them, because He knew all men, and had no need that anyone should testify of man, for He knew what was in man." From this passage we can observe the following: Christ was focused, He knew his audience, He wasn't overly concerned about man's opinion about Him, He understood His mission, and He had discernment.

According to John 12:49–50, Christ also knew God's agenda, and this agenda was His agenda as well. He was not seeking to do what He wanted; He wanted to do what the Father wanted. Christ also utilized a "listen (Father to Son) and then speak" (Son to man) method of instruction.

We find in John 16:12–15 that Christ models the greatest principle concerning working with teens. Christ didn't use technology or theology in his teaching. He used parables and illustrations taken from the culture of those whom He was addressing. He packaged the truth so that the audience would understand it. Christ would then move to deeper truths. Christ was dependent upon the Holy Spirit as He ministered truths to those around Him.

Christ employed various study methods to help His disciples understand, as seen in Matthew 17:24–27:

> When they had come to Capernaum, those who received the temple tax came to Peter and said, "Does your Teacher not pay the temple tax?" He said, "Yes." And when he had come into the house, Jesus anticipated him, saying, "What do you think, Simon? From whom do the kings of the earth take customs or taxes, from their sons or from strangers?" Peter said to Him, "From strangers." Jesus said to him, "Then the sons are free. Nevertheless, lest we offend them, go to the sea, cast in a hook, and take the fish that comes up first. And when you have opened its mouth, you will find a piece of money; take that and give it to them for Me and you.

Here Christ utilizes the question-and-answer method with Peter. Christ asked a provocative question, forcing Peter to think through his answer. Additionally Christ utilized a visual aid; a teachable moment, assignment, and application helping Peter to understand the problem at hand.

Additional methods employed by Christ included:

1. He asked questions (to Nicodemus in John 3:1–15, and to the woman at the well in John 4:1–26).
2. He recognized the personal worth of individuals (Luke 19:2–10).
3. He used word pictures from everyday life (Luke 13:19).
4. He taught by example (John 13:1–17).
5. He knew Scripture (Matthew 4:1–11).
6. He showed genuine emotion (John 11:35–36).
7. He prayed for His followers (John 17).
8. He spent quality and quantity time with the twelve (Mark 1:17–20; 6:30–31).
9. He made use of silence (John 8:1–11, Luke 23:9).
10. He utilized specific instructions (Matthew 11:20–36).

THE TEACHING AND LEARNED GAP

A funny thing happens when we ask teachers and students to evaluate the teaching performances.

Mostly there is a "gap" between the teachers' actual performance and the desired goals. Impactful teaching calls for and demands disciplined study and proper planning of each lesson. Thus, thoughtful, disciplined preparation is essential for improved teaching. The better the preparation, the greater the margin for success. The teacher who is disciplined in planning each lesson will eventually benefit from a greater satisfaction in teaching. Diligent, thoughtful preparation of each lesson produces the most effective teaching for both the teacher and the students.

BASIS FOR CHOOSING TEACHING METHODS
Age of Your Class

The age of your group is one of the most important concerns of your teaching. For our purposes, we will break the youth into three age groups: early (10–12 years), middle, (13–17 years), and late (18–24 years). Each group has its own needs.

1. **Early Youth.** The early age group (10–12 years) tends to do things in two separate groups, guys against girls.
2. **Middle Youth.** The middle group (13–17 years) becomes interested in doing things together as a group. Most teens hang out in groups as couples and as friends. Individuals are interested in the opposite sex but enjoy doing things together if they are planned in an informal way. This age group is most critical, and their thinking is greatly governed by the latest fashions, music, magazines, and TV. Cliques are more of a problem, so you must plan your lessons to work away from these cliques and toward a Christian goal. Much prayer is needed to analyze this age group and to know how to meet their needs.
3. **Late Youth.** The late group (18–24) consists largely of couples and college students. They have completely different needs. You need to plan more intellectual programs with a logical aim behind everything that is said and done.

Needs of Your Class

What are the needs of your group? Have you considered what would best meet the immediate needs of the teens you are ministering to? If not, stop now and do so before your organization grows less interesting or you lose another young person. Are they being taught how to be future leaders, Sunday school teachers, presidents of groups, or church leaders? Perhaps a study in leadership, unity, or dating ethics would be good material for your class's next study series.

Have you tried making a mental or written list of the needs of your group? Keeping these needs in mind will produce a better method of presentation. Needs determine the method of approach. You will find that the needs of your group will vary with environment. Economic, social, and educational background—each of these must be considered before choosing a method of presentation. At no time in history has the needs of today's adolescents been more varied or complex. Your lesson material must meet the needs of the youth under your care.

Needs of Your Students

Consider the needs of the individuals within your group. Each of these individuals differs completely from all the others. Their makeup is different. Their needs are different. This extends into the life of every teen in every area—physically, mentally, morally, socially, and emotionally. Have you noticed any peculiar characteristics of an individual as he appears in a group? Have you visited his home? If you haven't, do so. When you are planning a lesson, remember you are ministering to needs of individuals within a group. You must consider the individual needs of every student. You must gear your teaching to meet some need in the student's life—both those who are popular and the loner in the back of the room. Your teaching must meet these needs, whatever they are. This means that a relationship must be formed.

Enthusiasm of Your Students

What about the enthusiasm in your group as you prepare to lecture? Are some of the students asleep or talking so that you cannot get their attention? Maybe you should try some other method of presentation. Ask your teens which type of presentation they like best. Unless your method is interesting, you will soon lose their attention and lose the student. Let your teens and their needs be your guide in the methods you choose. You will find age-group needs and individuals' needs entering into the picture as you plan what method to use. With the ever-increasing presence of technology, there is no excuse for us not to create an environment of enthusiasm using cutting-edge media and presentation packaging. As you meet the needs of students in your group, a natural enthusiasm will develop.

FACILITIES AT HAND

Set the Environment

Every student is affected by the atmosphere. Professional sports teams battle to carry "home field advantage" during the play-offs. Why? Because the hometown fans create an environment of excitement and anticipation. Many professional athletes will comment that they "feed" off the excitement and energy of the crowd. It helps them to perform better.

Likewise, the teacher must take care that his environment for study is conducive to do just that, study. Setting the proper environment is accomplished through the following:

Establish the material surroundings. The surroundings in which the teacher prepares greatly influences the quality of his preparation. Zeal for study, attitudes toward students, quality of preparation, and tone of prayer are all affected by the physical surroundings. These factors all influence (positively and negatively) the quality of the lesson plan. Make no mistake, preparation and study are exhausting and take intellectual effort. So any distraction or disturbance decreases the quality of the lesson plan and distracts from its overall effectiveness in developing the lesson. In addition to an environment of uninterrupted contemplation, the "study" itself must be well equipped. Furnishings, lighting, and materials (books, pens, paper, etc.) must be arranged in such a way to help facilitate the teacher's study. This takes planning and thoughtful consideration of the surroundings.

Pray that the Holy Spirit will enlighten and grant insight. This aspect of prayer is overlooked or totally ignored by many teachers and in fact, demonstrates a lack of dependence on God and the Holy Spirit. The teacher who fails to pray before, during, and after lesson preparation is preparing for failure and inviting disaster into the classroom. Since teaching Scripture is a spiritual/supernatural matter, teachers are mandated to depend and "lean on" the One who guides, convicts, and leads us into all spiritual truth. Further, the teacher who fails to seek the help of the Holy Spirit in the preparation fails to experience the joy of working in fellowship with Him. What better peace is there than knowing that the same Spirit who inspired the authors of Scripture will assist in helping the teacher prepare and present the same Book. A teacher's preparation must include prayer for guidance and insight. As teachers of Scripture, we will be held accountable for our teaching of the Word (James 3:1). We are dealing with people and issues that have eternal consequences that can be affected by the quality of our message. This responsibility must be taken seriously.

Pray over the class. The effective teacher teaches to the needs of the students. Praying over the class goes hand in hand with the above point. As I pray over my students, considering their situations and spiritual condition, I will be better equipped to structure activities and lessons toward those needs. As I pray for dependence and guidance from the Holy Spirit, I am relying on His help to structure the lesson content and the words of my mouth to be as effective as possible. This is where the supernatural aspect comes into play. As teachers, if we pray for the Holy Spirit's help in revealing insight, truth, and creativity, and communication to us, He will help. God wants our students to be saved and conformed to His image more than we do.

Equipment. Having the proper equipment—chalk, chalkboard, maps, pictures, overhead projection equipment, PowerPoint, AV equipment, etc.—is vital. The facilities at hand will largely determine what methods will be used. The more tools to choose from, the greater the end result.

Time. You must have adequate time to present the material using the method you have chosen. Something that is not finished during one class or meeting period will not hold interest later. You as a leader are responsible for limiting your presentation to the time allotted. Remember, going overtime is not the answer to a program that has too much content. Interest is lost when your time is up. Make sure you quit before your students do.

Place. Do you have sufficient room for your presentation? Is the seating capacity sufficient for your audience? If they are crowded together, interest will be harder to hold. Is the room adequately ventilated, lighted, and heated? All these things must be considered if you are to be an effective teacher.

The Aim of Your Class

What is the objective of your time together? Is it just to fill up time, to entertain, or to hold interest? Or is it geared to meet a need in the lives of the teens? Every meeting, small or large, should have a purpose. Your purpose should always be to meet the needs of your group. The method and purpose should fit together perfectly.

The Spiritual Level of Your Class

If you consider your group a relatively immature one, then you have an idea as to some of the needs of the group. You may now plan a class and use methods of presenting the need for a life dedicated to Christ. Do not try to teach an immature group as you would a mature group because you will not be meeting their immediate needs.

Then again, if your class is a spiritually mature group who is living for Christ, you have the opportunity to lead them into a deeper spiritual knowledge of God. This group will probably have resourceful individuals. Planned responsibility may help the youth gain experiences that they may use as they become the leaders of the church. Use methods that will apply to your group, and consider whether they are carnal, new babes, rededicated, or Spiritual Christians.

Master the Passage

There is a marked difference between understanding what the lesson is and what the lesson is actually about. It is never enough to know what the curriculum writers or what the commentaries have to say about a given passage or lesson. It is imperative that the teacher masters the Bible passage. To master the Bible passage, two things must be accomplished: 1) A complete knowledge of the Bible passage must be achieved. This will include the specific passage itself and any "background" information on the given passage. 2) Clear, understandable lesson aims must be formulated that correlate to the material structure. These two areas are paramount to formulating and presenting a high-impact lesson. The teacher may have an excellent understanding of Scripture but not know how to arrange a lesson for effective teaching. The following steps will help the teacher to master the lesson passage.

1. **Read the Passage Three to Five Times.**
   Nothing decodes a Bible passage as well as reading it over and over. While reading the passage, the teacher

should be praying that the Holy Spirit will enlighten and reveal insights that will meet the needs of the students. As one reads and rereads Scripture, one cannot help but to think and meditate on that passage. This leads to making observations and interpretations that otherwise would be missed. The more that Scriptures consume the mind and thought process of the teacher, the more effective that person will be in presenting the lesson. Lessons become more "real" to the students if they are first "real" to the teacher. It is the difference between a meaningful, self-discovered lesson and one that has been handed down from a third source. This practice of reading through the lesson passage should transpire each day preceding the teaching. The teacher will want to read the passage prayerfully and meditatively, looking for observations, the human element, key words, key ideas, and key persons.

The teacher should develop his own system for marking these key elements and cross-referencing the passage. In addition, the teacher should use a dictionary to look up any unfamiliar definitions and pronunciations. For additional understanding, the teacher should read different translations and versions of the passage. A Bible dictionary is helpful for understanding the cultural events that surround the passage. The reading and rereading of the passage should continue until the passage becomes so alive and real that the teaching of it is a "release" for the teacher and a delight for the students.

2. **Outline the Passage**
   After the teacher is familiar with the passage, he should write a brief outline of the passage. Break the passage down into three to five main points with corresponding sub points. This outline may be used during the lesson and reinforces the teacher's understanding of the logical flow of the passage.

3. **Understand the setting and history of the passage.**
   As mentioned previously, the teacher would be wise to gain as much understanding of the background of the passage as possible. This would include author, date, culture, audience, and geography. These aspects all play a part in understanding the passage.

   Not all of this information is necessary in the presentation of the lesson. It will simply better equip the teacher in planning and preparation, thus giving the Holy Spirit a greater "network" of information to draw from as the teacher prepares and presents the lesson.

4. **Summarize the Lesson**
   Writing out a brief summary of the lesson will benefit the teacher. A summary consists of the broad contents of the lesson. At this point the teacher should not include details, applications, or background material. This step is intended to simply help the teacher clarify and organize the material by forcing him or her to state the lesson in a clear and concise way.

5. **Verify Conclusions**
   Commentaries and books can verify and support the teacher's own "self discovery" and conclusions formed during the personal Bible Study time. Warning: Don't let commentaries and books become a crutch for your thinking. The danger here is when commentaries and books cause the teacher to abandon the working of the Holy Spirit in and through the personal Bible Study.

As spiritual shepherds, we would be wise to model the teaching methods of Christ with our students. In addition, we should understand the working of the Holy Spirit as we prepare and teach the Word of God, relating biblical truth that will meet the needs of our students and equip them for a life of service for Christ.

WHY DO YOU BELIEVE THAT?

Alex McFarland

> We already <u>know</u> that we're not supposed to take drugs, have sex, or drop out of school. Sometimes adults think we're just a bunch of goofballs, only interested in pizza and concerts. But kids in our youth group really do want to learn all about Christianity, and what the Bible says. We want to be taught God's Word, and we're ready for it.
>
> Allison, 11th grade Christian teen, New Jersey[1]

The September morning air felt cold as I walked from my car toward the flagpole. Across the school property in front of me, I was encouraged by the large gathering of students in front of the building. *Wow . . . a pretty impressive group at this hour*, I thought as I glanced at my watch. It was "See You At The Pole" day, and a group of students from this particular high school had asked me to attend and speak.

Groups of students were all around the flagpole—talking, laughing, and occasionally shivering. From one conversation, I overheard a question that made my heart heavy: "Why do Christians think that everybody who doesn't agree with them is going to hell?" I had been invited to "SYATP" by members of an after-school Christian club, but something I saw told me that they were not the only campus group present. A banner held by several teens read, "Intolerance At The Pole." I could see one teen offering a Christian booklet to a person helping hold up the sign. It turns out that members of the school's "Diversity

111

Club" had also gotten up early, coming to the flagpole to make a statement about *their* views. I was glad to see that many of the Christian teens seemed to be extending a friendly welcome. I caught the sound of another question: "Why are Christians always trying to force their *opinions* on other people?"

We had met at the flagpole to pray, and I was already talking to the Lord while the youth leader was introducing me. Looking back, I see that experience as a prime example of why Christians today should become familiar with *apologetics*.

In verses such as Matthew 28:18–20 and Mark 16:15, God instructed believers of all ages to present the message of Jesus Christ to the people around them. It takes personal effort, dedication, and commitment in order to do this effectively. Evangelism today (and especially youth ministry) can be enhanced by knowledge of apologetics as we share and explain Christianity.

APOLOGETICS: A BASIC DEFINITION

Within the North American church, the term *Christian apologetics* is still new to many people. In short, apologetics is the practice of presenting *reasons for what you believe*. Apologetics deal with *what we believe and why*. Most Christians who have witnessed to unbelievers have probably heard various objections to the gospel message. Some people may have heard that the Bible contains errors. Others wonder how God (if He exists) could have allowed the recent tsunamis and hurricanes to happen. Whether a listener has a legitimate question about God or responds with a thinly veiled excuse, a basic knowledge of apologetics is vitally important for Christians today. We should equip ourselves and our students to give a knowledgeable answer and to support our faith convincingly.

> **a-pol'o-get'ics,** *n.;* the discipline which deals with a rational defense of Christianity; giving a reason or justification of one's beliefs; use of evidence and sound reasoning to reach individuals for Christ.[2]

Apologetics means "a defense," and this word occurs several times in the Bible.[3] When we do apologetics, we are defending what we believe by showing that the content of the gospel is "backed up" by both evidence and sound reasoning.

First Peter 3:15 (NIV) encourages believers to, "be prepared to give an answer to everyone who asks you to give the reason for the hope that you have." In short, we are told to "back up" why we have faith. The words translated "answer" and "reason" are ancient terms, implying "analysis," "consideration of one's position," and the "defense of a conclusion."[4] A similar wording is found in Philippians 1:7,17, where Paul said that he was prepared to defend the gospel. The principle is echoed in Jude 3, as believers are encouraged to "contend earnestly" (or "stand up for") the faith.

OVERVIEW OF CHANGES IN AMERICA AND THE WEST

Americans today live in a nation plagued by a chronic decline in morals and erosion of the basic values and principles on which our nation was founded. We have moved away from our Judeo-Christian roots and into a world characterized by relativism and corruption. To understand fully where much of Western culture is today, we must examine changes that brought us to where we are.

Historically, the enlightenment period was the beginning of the end of the Judeo-Christian worldview in the West. From the early 1600s through the 1700s, society experienced a revolution of sorts. People began relying on rational thought rather than religious faith to discern truth. This led to widespread acceptance of *empiricism* (the belief that unless something could be tested, it isn't real) as the ultimate test for truth. As a result, religious truth claims were considered invalid, merely a matter of personal opinion, because they could not be empirically proven or verified. *Modernism* emerged out of this enlightenment perspective, a belief that rational thought and scientific verification are the only true pathways to knowledge.

Some eventually found the cold and impersonal nature of modernism undesirable. As people became disillusioned with rationalism, *romanticism* emerged in response to this disillusionment. Romanticism carried with it a shift in the view of humanity. Not only did Romanticists view nature as the highest good, but they also saw humanity as essentially good, rather than as sinful. Romanticists attempted to ignore the inconsistency in a society where widespread corruption coexisted with "naturally good" humans. However, people eventually understood the discrepancy between romanticism and reality, so a new worldview was needed to explain this discrepancy.

Disillusionment with both romanticism and modernism would ultimately contribute to the emergence of *postmodernism*. Because neither romanticism nor modernism was able to answer with certainty the answers to the big questions of life, postmodernists concluded that *no* answers existed. Postmodernism asserts that no one answer can be better or more right than another. According to postmodernists, claiming that your answer is the right answer is both arrogant and intolerant. Our postmodern world is one based on constantly shifting standards of right and wrong, in which there is no such thing as absolute truth. Those setting forth fixed, absolute judgments about reality or morality (such as Christians) are dismissed as being intolerant.

The pervasive postmodernist assumes that truth is either nonexistent or may, personally defined, pose a serious threat to young people, particularly if they do not know why they believe what they believe. For this reason, apologetics continues to grow in its scope and relevancy to today's world. Apologetics is, in fact, the first step in bringing our society back from moral decay.

No one who knows the world as it is today can deny that it is skeptical and cold, either indifferent to, or furiously antagonistic against the doctrines of the Christian faith . . . The children in many cases grow up to be ignorant of the creed of the church, and when they go off to college are ready to be swept along by Darwinism, Buddhism, Christian Science, or any other insanity or delusion of the hour.

Charles E. Jefferson, 1908[5]

THE RISE OF APOLOGETICS

Christians (who today would be identified as conservatives or evangelicals) in America and Europe were well aware of developments of the nineteenth (and late eighteenth) centuries, which were seen as intellectual threats to Christianity. Published in 1799, Frederick Schleiermacher's (1768–1834) book *On Religion* defined religion in terms of personal subjective experience over objective, propositional truth. A later work entitled *The Christian Faith* further defined authentic Christianity in terms of "consciousness of dependence on God." Sometimes referred to as "the father of German liberalism," Schleiermacher conflicted with biblical orthodoxy at a number of points, not the least of which was his rejection of Christ's Deity. His influence played a significant role in the drift away from biblical orthodoxy that occurred in the Western world throughout the 1800s.[6]

Both inside and outside of the church, the view of God as "communicator" eroded during the nineteenth century, as doubts about the Bible grew. Charles Darwin's *On the Origin of the Species*, published in 1859, undermined the view of God as Creator. In the minds of many, there grew an increasing conviction that religious *faith* and empirical *fact* were separate, unrelated phenomena, which did not need to reconcile. Beginning in the 1800s, several influential individuals began to popularize the concept that a distinction should be maintained between the Jesus people *believe in* and the person who Jesus literally *was*. Though using similar terminologies in subtly different ways, the influence of individuals like David Strauss (1808–1874), Gotthold Lessing (1729–1781), and Martin Kahler (1835–1912) led many to accept the concept that belief and history are (of necessity) based on different foundations; distinctions between *personal faith* and *historical realities* must consistently be maintained. In the early twentieth century, writings like Albert Schweitzer's 1906 book, *The Quest of the Historical Jesus*, continued to popularize the idea that the "Christ of faith" and the "Jesus of history" are two different persons.[7] As the twentieth century dawned, Christianity in the Western world was simultaneously critiqued, assaulted, and revised, and such challenges would only intensify in the decades ahead.

The apologetics movement of today may be traced to leaders who, over one hundred years ago, emerged in defense of Christianity. Though liberalism and revisionism were (and are) academically fashionable, those defending key points of Christian orthodoxy certainly made their voices heard. Charles Hodges defended Genesis and the biblical account of creation in his 1878 work, *What Is Darwinism?* Benjamin Warfield (a professor at Princeton Seminary from 1887 until his death in 1921) was a scholarly defender of the Bible and a vocal critic of liberalism.

A major development for conservative theology and apologetics in America began in 1909. Two Christian businessmen funded the research and writing of a series of essays designed to defend the "essentials" of Christian doctrine and to effectively respond to liberalism (then often called "modernism"). The articles were written by conservative scholars of the day, including Benjamin Warfield, C.I. Scofield, G. Campbell Morgan, James Orr, and others.[8]

The resulting ninety articles and essays addressed many topics related to apologetics and Christian orthodoxy. Topics included the inspiration and preservation of the Bible, the virgin birth and deity of Christ, the reality of Jesus' miracles and resurrection, and more. Christian leader Reuben A. Torrey (educated at Yale Divinity School and later president of Moody Bible Institute) edited the articles into a four-volume set titled *The Fundamentals.* Three million free copies of *The Fun-*

damentals were printed and sent to ministers and Christians throughout America.

In recent years, the term "fundamentalist" has developed a very negative connotation. Screaming street preachers and Islamic terrorists are each labeled "fundamentalists." The term has more than lost the meaning it carried initially (which was actually a *complimentary* description of one who affirmed the tenets of biblical orthodoxy). "Fundamentalist" is now considered a very negative, pejorative term, and it is no longer part of the evangelical world's "preferred vocabulary." But the books which once carried that name did much to help people understand that Christianity was reasonable and credible.

LATTER TWENTIETH-CENTURY DEVELOPMENTS IN CHRISTIAN APOLOGETICS

During the twentieth century, liberal theology, cultural trends, and conservative Christianity clashed on numerous (and often well-publicized) occasions. In the struggle for (or against) biblical orthodoxy, lines were drawn within colleges, denominations, and local churches. The quest for theological purity saw the birth of new colleges and seminaries (such as Westminster Seminary and Dallas Theological Seminary in the 1920s). The 1925 "Monkey Trial" (concerning teacher John T. Scopes and his presentation of evolution in the Dayton, Tennessee public schools) vividly presented the conflict between biblical content and emerging culture.

Despite the positive intellectual momentum gathered by Christians during the early 1900s, the Scopes Trial marked the beginning of a period in which conservative Christianity in American was perceived as being "anti-intellectual." A marked lack of modern scholarship used in defending creationism (and Christianity as a whole) during the trials led to negative press and eventually to a shift of focus from key issues to peripheral ones. Liberalism won back lost ground, gained momentum, and damaged evangelical influence in mainline churches. Some evangelicals defeated themselves by reducing their intellectual pursuits and accomplishments to quibbles over nitpicky, secondary issues.

OBSERVATIONS FROM AN APOLOGETICS PIONEER

"When I entered Bible college in 1950, there were only two books available written by contemporary apologists," says Dr. Norman Geisler. "Fortunately, there are now hundreds of good apologetics resources in print." Geisler speaks authoritatively when recounting the growth of apologetics in the latter twentieth century. As a speaker, educator, and prolific apologetics writer, Geisler's influence has been tremendous from the 1960s to the present day. Geisler witnessed the emergence of modern apologetics firsthand, and he remains a contributing participant:

> When I started in ministry, John Carnell's book *Christian Apologetics* (1951) and *The Christian View of God and Man* by James Orr were the main books available. Later, Francis Schaeffer's writings began to cause Christians to think about world-view issues, many for the first time. We also began to get books written by this guy from England who had spoken on the BBC, and who we had all heard about. Though they had been written years before, it wasn't until the early 1960s that most of us in American apologetics got our first copies of *Miracles, The Problem of Pain,* and *Mere Christianity*—and became familiar with C.S. Lewis.[9]

Of the more than sixty books that Geisler has written, many are standard texts in Christian colleges and graduate programs, and many are considered modern-day apologetics classics. In 2002, Baker Book House published Geisler's *Encyclopedia of Christian Apologetics.* An unprecedented work of over eight hundred pages, production of this book alone would have demonstrated Geisler's impact on modern apologetics. By the end of 2004, Geisler had also completed and released a three-volume, apologetic-based systematic theology—devoting over two thousand pages to the subjects of God, the Bible, and creation.

A TIME OF RISING VISIBILITY FOR APOLOGETICS

By the 1970s, young Christian leaders like Ravi Zacharias, W. David Beck, Winfried Corduan, David Clark, J. P. Moreland, Gary Habermas, William Lane Craig, and others took on the mantle of apologetics.

"Josh McDowell deserves credit for taking the message to campuses all over the nation, and popularizing apologetics," says Geisler.[10] Christian organizations that focused specifically on apologetics (such as PROBE, Search Ministries, and Dr. David Noebel's Summit Ministries) began to train many Christians to think in terms of apologetics and a biblical worldview. By the 1980s, notable Christian Colleges (such as Wheaton College and Liberty University) were offering courses and degree programs in apologetics.

Since the 1970s, hundreds of apologetics books have been released in America, ranging from scholarly treatments of specialized subjects to more practical and popular overview-type "handbooks." Countless Americans have been introduced to the world of apologetics through books like Josh McDowell's *More Than a Carpenter* (with over ten million copies in print) and *Evidence That Demands a Verdict* (parts I and II). More recently, lawyer Lee Strobel's award-winning books, *The Case for Christ* and *The Case for a Creator*, have introduced apologetics to a brand new generation.

THE RELEVANCY OF APOLOGETICS

Why apologetics teaching is important for teens

Many American teenagers demonstrate a clear lack of knowledge regarding their faith and the issues surrounding it.

Especially in a society where biblical truths and Christian precepts are consistently challenged and attacked, it is crucial that we address this lack of knowledge and bring our nation's youth into a place of understanding where they are rationally and truthfully able to give a reason for what they believe.

> Teens are largely unprepared for the assault on faith that college will bring. Prepared or not, college students will face questions like, "Is there a God?" and "If God exists, what's Her name?" We know of many students whose faiths crumbled during their college years, through doubt, bad decisions, and unwise choices in friendships. I think that all of these situations could have been avoided if the students were just better equipped to handle life outside of their parents, and life apart from their church. More and more, when a student graduates from high school, they've also graduated from church.
>
> Mark Smith, youth pastor, North Carolina[11]

Sixty-two percent of those under age thirty question the ability of religion to influence life in America anymore,[12] and almost 80 percent of teens will no longer participate in organized religion/church by the time they reach adulthood.[13] The number of students who are turning from their faiths demonstrates their ill-preparedness for living out their Christianity in a hostile society. Apologetics for teens is the cure, or rather the vaccination, for this growing concern because it will provide students with the tools and knowledge that they need to defend, explain, and understand their faiths.

Because a majority of teens aren't sure that moral absolutes exist,[14] or even that you can be sure that any one religion is right,[15] apologetics continues to grow in its scope and relevancy to teenagers today. Apologetics for teens is designed to help them understand what it really means to have a Christian worldview and to equip them to answer the challenges they will undoubtedly face at school, with their friends, and possibly even in the home.

Teaching our teens apologetics alone will not transform their lives—only a personal relationship with the Lord Jesus Christ can accomplish that. But presentation and explanation of Christian content is vitally important in a culture so full of non-biblical messages. Knowledge of apologetics will provide Christian students with the ability to "always be prepared to give an answer to everyone who asks you to give the reason for the hope that you have" (1 Peter 3:15 NIV).

Rob Dennis, a youth minister now serving in Connecticut, began incorporating apologetics teaching into his youth ministry shortly after 9/11. Not long after the attacks, students began to ask Dennis questions about Islam. He explains, "It's not enough to just tell youth 'The Bible says so, and the church says so.' Teens want to understand their Christian faith and the reasons behind it."[16]

Dennis is now serving New Life Church in Meriden, Connecticut, along with founding pastor Will Marrotti. About 350 of New Life's 400 members are new believers, reached since the church began in 1999. Dennis says, "We teach basic apologetics because Christian kids (and many of their non-Christian friends) have questions . . . so many questions."[17]

Rob Dennis, Mark Smith, and many other youth ministers emphasize the importance of maintaining an environment where students feel free to ask questions. Dennis asserts,

The things that come up in discussions show that they are thinking, and really seeking truth that makes sense. How do we know that Jesus is the only way to God? How can we be sure that the Bible is really accurate? Why is God so against homosexuality if people really love each other? What if Jesus really didn't rise from the grave? How do we know there is a heaven, and what will it be like? These types of issues are only the tip of the iceberg.[18]

THE ROLE OF APOLOGETICS

Each believer has the assignment of not only presenting the gospel, but also explaining and defending the truths of our message. Fortunately, there is plenty of evidence to support what we believe. Christianity tells us that Jesus loved us, and His authenticity is proven by the fact that He came back to life after dying. The Bible reminds us that the good news about Jesus is not just based on human opinion or personal preference. Christianity is *truth*. Second Peter 1:16 reminds us that the message of Jesus was not based on fables or myths. Romans 1:4 says that Jesus' resurrection shows that He was the unique Son of God. (Think about it. How many other people in history have—under their own power—gone to "the other side" and come back?) Acts 1:3 says that after His resurrection, Christ showed that He was alive by many undeniable proofs.

Christianity is unique in that it is the only faith system based on facts of history that can be investigated. Many people today risk eternity by trusting their own opinion about what it means to be in right relation to God. In contrast to this, Christianity alone is based upon historically verifiable words and events. When a non-Christian says, "You have no right to judge me," they are absolutely correct. But Jesus has evaluated the entire human race, and His Word sums it up for each of us: "You must be born again" (John 3:7).

Categories of Christian apologetics include: *Textual apologetics*—defending the trustworthiness of the Bible and then sharing the content of what it says; *Evidence-based apologetics*—presenting the many evidences in defense of the Christian faith (such as facts from history or science); and *Philosophical apologetics*—exposing the flawed reasoning behind many of the popular arguments against Christianity. Respected Christian thinkers throughout history (such as Thomas Aquinas) have recognized that every argument against Christianity is rooted in faulty logic and incorrect conclusions.

A fourth area of apologetics relates not to external facts or evidences, but to our own character and behavior as a believer—*Practical apologetics*. Christians may *know* apologetics, and Christians may *do* apologetics, but we must also remember that as a new creature in Christ, each believer *is* an apologetic.

THE LIMITS OF APOLOGETICS

We should keep in mind that apologetics must never be simply facts and data stored in our brains; apologetics should also be "truth lived out in consistency and love." We must turn our apologetics knowledge into what authors Josh McDowell and Dave Bellis term *relational apologetics*. Biblical truth, sound reasoning, or compelling data carry little weight unless they are presented by an authentic messenger whose life has been genuinely changed. Josh McDowell states: "Human relational connections and deepened convictions about God are intertwined. Thus, if we are going to deepen our young people's convictions about a God who is passionate about relationships, we need to form strong, positive relational connections with them."[19] McDowell explains the caring, consistent Christian example that leaders are challenged to model before teens:

> When I talk about entering their world, I'm not talking about trying to live like preteens or teenagers—dressing like them, talking like them, listening to their music, and so on. I mean taking an interest and being aware of what's happening in their lives and then relationally connecting with them as Christ the Incarnate One models for us—accepting them without condition, loving them sacrificially, affirming them in their struggles and victories, and being available to them always. When you make that kind of connection with the young people in your life, you ready their hearts for the relational connection God wants to have with them through His Son Jesus Christ.[20]

Facts and data are important; and among the world's belief systems, Christianity is unique in its empirical corroboration. Apologetic evidences can be very potent ministry tools, in both "reaching and teaching." But apologetics is no substitute for prayer (we must intercede on behalf of the lost, and not just assume that proofs and evidence will draw the unsaved to Christ). In terms of evangelism, apologetics do not override God's sovereign timetable or human will. The persuasiveness of a presentation is not the deciding factor in whether or not someone accepts Christ. The focal points of our evangelistic approach should be the finished work of Christ, the content of the gospel, and the power of the Holy Spirit to draw and to convert.

Finally, apologetics is no substitute for a godly, yielded life. Ability to "defend the faith" comes with the responsibility to "live the faith." Apologist and author David Clark states: "A commitment to defending the faith is not a promise to argue whatever, however, whenever, and with whomever. It is a commitment to be, to the highest degree possible, what God wants His servants to be—intellectually, relationally, and spiritually."[21] Clark sums it up well by reminding all aspiring apologists, "Who you are counts most."[22]

The way that we act, react, and live daily should complement the words that we speak. Christians must truly live out their faith, yielded to the leading of God's Spirit and the parameters of God's Word. Otherwise, we lose the power of our witness, no matter how deeply bolstered by reasoning or facts.

APOLOGETICS IN YOUTH MINISTRY

Christian apologetics is both a useful and crucial tool for use in student ministry. Youth will appreciate the growth in their own faith as they learn the reasons and truths behind their beliefs. They also would be grateful for the opportunity to share with their friends what they believe in a rational and reasonable way, particularly because they most likely face peers and teachers who challenge their faith on a consistent basis. Youth leaders should be equipped to teach their teens to become effective apologists; however, the vast scope and depth of Christian beliefs makes introducing apologetics to youth a daunting undertaking. It will help to understand the key issues, objectives, and functions as related to Christian apologetics.

As a youth pastor or leader, there are several predominant issues and topics that should be addressed. They include:

- The existence, nature, character, and attributes of God
- God's revelation, and the fact that He has shown Himself to the world
- Truth (and epistemology, which deals with the question of how we know anything)
- The Bible and how we can be sure of its veracity
- Jesus Christ, His divinity and humanity, and the evidence that verifies that He rose from the dead
- Answering the problem of evil
- The credibility of the biblical miracles
- The Judeo-Christian heritage of both Western culture and of the United States
- The absolute (fixed) nature of morality
- Responding to non-Christian religions, cults, and the occult

Rather than simply describing these key issues, youth leaders should address them with an eye toward the fulfillment of several basic objectives. These objectives include presenting, explaining, and defending the Christian message—to prove that Christianity is credible, understandable, and urgent (that is, "requires a response"). Incorporation of apologetics into evangelism and youth ministry is done in light of Christ's Great Commission, seeking to see the lost masses converted, biblically literate, and committed to the Lordship of Christ.

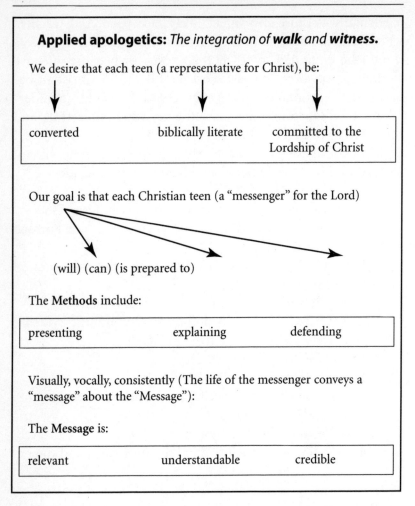

Applied apologetics: *The integration of **walk** and **witness**.*

We desire that each teen (a representative for Christ), be:

| converted | biblically literate | committed to the Lordship of Christ |

Our goal is that each Christian teen (a "messenger" for the Lord)

(will) (can) (is prepared to)

The **Methods** include:

| presenting | explaining | defending |

Visually, vocally, consistently (The life of the messenger conveys a "message" about the "Message"):

The **Message** is:

| relevant | understandable | credible |

Christian teens should be equipped to live out the biblical injunction of 2 Peter 1:16 and of Jude 3: being able to defend one's faith. Adult leaders must alert teens of their responsibilities to present, explain, and defend the faith, and equip the teens for this. Finally, apologetics teaching is intended to encourage believers to not only know Christian truth, but also to convey that truth to those around them.

THE RESULT OF APOLOGETICS

Teens in our nation and world hold beliefs that range from the secular to the spiritual. Beliefs and religions include everything from *atheism* (belief that there is no God), to *polytheism* (belief in multiple gods). But regardless of the label that describes an individual's view of the world, an effective presentation of the gospel often requires that we talk to the individual about certain assumptions they may hold. Before students may be willing to consider what Jesus taught, we may have to help them over some mental barriers that stand in their way. In a culture known for its rejection of authority and a "prove it to me" attitude, knowledge of apologetics is a vital help in reaching and teaching teens and adults.

Excellent books on apologetics are available by authors like Josh McDowell, Lee Strobel, Ravi Zacharias, Gary Habermas, Norman Geisler, and many others. Good resources are essential to the process of becoming equipped for effective Christian witness. When someone is ready to trust Christ, and appears to have no objections standing in the way, there may be no need to talk about peripheral issues. But for an increasingly skeptical culture such as ours, Christians should rise to the challenge of 1 Peter 3:15 and "always be ready."

I began this chapter with my experience at a local high school during a "See You At The Pole" gathering. As I addressed the students, the tension faded as both groups listened with interest to some facts I shared concerning apologetics. "The words of the Bible and the record of history both tell us about Jesus and what He taught," I told the crowd. The fall breeze brought gentle noises from the leaves on a nearby tree, and from the flag suspended above our heads. "Please remember this," I said. "Christianity is not just somebody's *opinion*. It is based on *facts*." Once again, I was reminded that students do want to be taught truth, and they have the capacity to understand far more than we give them credit.

NOTES

1. Interview with Christian teens, in discussion with the author, March, 2005.

2. This is the author's personal definition, developed through personal study and years of ministry around the nation.

3. W. E. Vine, *Vine's Expository Dictionary of New Testament Word* (published without copyright, 1940), 53.

4. Ibid., 924–925.

5. Charles Edward Jefferson, *The Minister As Prophet* (New York: Grosset and Dunlap, 1905), 178.

6. Earle E. Cairns, *Christianity Through The Centuries* (Grand Rapids, MI: Zondervan Publishing House, 1996), 419–420.

7. Martin Kahler, *The So-Called Historical Jesus and the Historic-Biblical Christ* (Philadelphia: Fortress Press, 1962) 43, 65–66.

David Strauss, *A New Life of Jesus*, 2nd ed. (London: Williams and Norgate, 1879). Albert Schweitzer, *The Quest of the Historical Jesus*, ed. John Bowden (Minneapolis, MN: Fortress Press, 2001).

Baker Encyclopedia of Christian Apologetics, ed. Norman L. Geisler (Grand Rapids, MI: Baker Books, 1999), s.v. "Christ of Faith vs. Jesus of History."

8. Michael E. Rusten and Sharon Rusten, ed. *When and Where In The Bible and Throughout History* (Wheaton, IL: Tyndale Publishers, 2005), 410.

9. Norman L. Geisler, in discussion with the author, May 2005.

10. Ibid.

11. Mark Smith, in discussion with the author, May 2005.

12. Pew Forum on Religion and Public Life: *Post 9–11 Attitudes* (December 6, 2001), 9.

13. Josh McDowell and Dave Bellis, *Beyond Belief: Partnering With the Church to Rebuild the Foundations of the Faith Within This Generation* (Wheaton, IL: Tyndale Publishers, 2002), 4.

14. Josh McDowell and Bob Hostetler, *The New Tolerance: How a Cultural Movement Threatens to Destroy You, Your Faith, and Your Children* (Wheaton, IL: Tyndale Publishers, 1998), 174.

15. Lee Weeks, "Teens Not Sure Christianity is Only Way," *Pulpit Helps* 26 no. 2 (2001): 1f.

16. Dennis Rob, in discussion with the author, May 2005.

17. Ibid.

18. Ibid.

19. Josh McDowell and Bob Hostetler, *Beyond Belief To Conviction: What You Need to Know to Help Youth Stand Strong in the Face of Today's Culture* (Wheaton, IL: Tyndale Publishers, 2002), 108.

20. Ibid., 114.

21. David K. Clark, *Dialogical Apologetics: A Person Centered Approach To Christian Defense* (Grand Rapids, MI: Baker Books, 1993), 234.

22. Ibid., 233.

THE "R" WORD THAT CHANGES YOUR MINISTRY

Calvin Carr

Do you have the latest methods for reaching students? Do you know the most effective way to reach teens through your church? Many church youth leaders and pastors feel compelled or sometimes even coerced to become trendy in order to reach the next generation of teenagers. The so-called experts say we must be radical in our music, youth meetings, and activities. We must make sure that students have fun and then walk away from our youth groups basking in the experience. Others purport that all youth leadership must be young in order to be culturally relevant and effective. Intrinsically, none of these things are wrong, but are they really criteria for success?

So what is the most important aspect of ministry for yielding lasting fruit? What is the most effective tool in the youth leader's arsenal? It happens in the context of building relationships. The youth pastor or leader who is willing to build strong relationships with other leaders and students will be the one who makes the greatest impact in youth ministry.

Dr. Oscar Thompson was a professor in the theology department at Southwestern Baptist Theological Seminary in Fort Worth, Texas. When I arrived at Southwestern, the ripple effect of his life was still obvious in many lives although he had recently died of cancer. He was a man who loved evangelism and challenged others to share their faith. Perhaps his greatest work in evangelism was a book he wrote titled *Concentric Circles of Concern.* In this book, he challenged believers to share the gospel in their personal concentric circles: home, extended family, work, and then acquaintances.

Many of the students remembered him asking this simple, yet powerful, question on every quiz or test he gave during the school year: "What's the most important word in the English language?" If you knew the answer to this question, then you were guaranteed at least a few points. What was the answer he was looking for? It was the word "relationships." Over my twenty-plus years of youth ministry, I have personally found this to be true. I would like to make the case that developing relationships is crucial to the success of student ministry.

It begins by creating a strategy for building relationships with both students and leaders. There must be a plan; you cannot depend on this happening by osmosis. It will not take place just because you run youth meetings or have a leadership team working with your students. It will happen on purpose because you make it a priority. Building relationships must be intentional!

There are some critical reasons for making the building of relationships a priority. First, we see this priority in the ministry of Jesus Christ. Jesus chose twelve disciples from the larger group that was following Him, "That they might be with Him" (see Mark 3:14 and Luke 6:13). Our Lord Jesus poured His life into these twelve men. This does not minimize the ministry He had with the crowds, but it does show how He spent extended time with His dedicated followers. He built an "up close and personal" relationship with them.

In Robert Coleman's classic book *The Master Plan of Evangelism*, he points out this simple methodology. From the beginning, we see Jesus giving each man a personal invitation which became the foundation of the relationship. John and Andrew were invited to come and see the place where Jesus stayed (John 1:39). Phillip was beckoned with two simple words, "Follow me" (John 1:43). Later when James, John, Peter, and Andrew were found mending their nets, Jesus used the same familiar words, "Follow Me, and I will make you fishers of men" (Matthew 4:19, Mark 1:17, and Luke 5:10).

"After Jesus chose the disciples, He devoted most of His remaining life on earth to those few men. He literally staked His whole ministry on them."[1] Jesus gave us the example of "being with" His disciples in every walk of life, and these same men eventually changed the world. One writer in *The Youth Leader's Sourcebook* put it this way: "Jesus was the disciples' ever-present model. He not only taught them by what He said, but He also taught them through what He did. I guess you can say He taught them audiovisually,"[2]

As a result of Jesus' ministry to these disciples, they were compelled to go into the known world with the gospel. Nearly every one of them sealed their commitment to Jesus with their own blood. They were martyrs for their faith. Men are not usually willing to die for a casual acquaintance. It was because of this deep, abiding relationship they shared with Christ that they were able to face death boldly.

Jesus Christ is not the only model of relationship building we see in the Scriptures. Other than our Savior, perhaps the apostle Paul is the premier example. Paul modeled this style of ministry and speaks of it clearly in 2 Timothy 2:2. Read his words and feel the conviction in his voice when he says, "And the things that you have heard from me among many witnesses, commit these to faithful men who will be able to teach others also."

Paul had a special relationship with young Timothy. He literally poured his life into young Timothy, who later became a pastor. We see it again in 1 Thessalonians 2:19 where Paul said, "For what is our hope, or joy, or crown of rejoicing? Is it not even you in the presence of our Lord Jesus Christ at His coming?" This type of influence cannot become a reality without building an intimate relationship with those in your ministry.

Think about the person who had the greatest ministry in your life. Or what about the person you feel you have truly impacted? You do not have to think very long before the pattern of relationship building will come into focus. Those whose lives we've really influenced are the ones with whom we've built relationships. Many years ago, Barry St. Clair spoke to nearly two hundred youth workers in our church. He taught us on this topic, and his comments could be summarized in these words: "It's not the programs that yield the greatest impact. Your youth program is merely the framework that allows godly youth workers to build relationships with teenagers. It is through these relationships that the real impression is made." In other words, "You can influence people from afar, but true impact is made up close."

This was demonstrated to me as a young seminary student in Texas. I had been asked by a large church in Dallas to come over and help with their youth ministry for the summer. They knew I had grown up in a large church and felt this experience would be valuable. They wanted me to serve in an interim position and minister to the students until the new youth minister arrived in August. Boy was I excited! This was going to be my chance to shine.

So what did I do? I scheduled every huge event possible. We had large activities all over the Dallas/Fort Worth area. I took the students to a professional baseball game, a rodeo, a water park, and a theme park, all the while thinking that I was a big-time youth minister.

During this very busy summer, my wife Kelly began to meet with a small group of girls in the home of one of the key families of the church. She had developed a friendship with one of the high school girls who volunteered to host this Bible study. I'll never forget the feeling I had when we left that large church. I felt as if I had been the busiest guy on the planet that summer. But as I looked at what Kelly had done, I realized that she had truly made a lasting difference in the lives of those girls. She developed a relationship with them, and the fruit showed in their lives.

Let me sound a word of caution here based on my tenure as

a youth pastor. If we are not careful, it is easy to develop student relationships that don't lead to much spiritual growth. We need to develop these relationships with the intent of leading students to spiritual growth. Students don't need just another friend, they need a leader.

This was obvious to me as a young college student at the University of Florida. I came back home for the summer to be a counselor at our annual youth camp. I remember our pastor, Dr. Homer G. Lindsay Jr., pulling some of us young guys aside and saying to us, "Boys, I know that you are excited about being counselors this year, but I want to make something very clear. These students don't need another friend; they need a leader."

That statement puzzled me at first, but after twenty years of youth ministry I now realize what he meant. He told us that what young people needed was a leader, someone who would guide them to be all that Christ wanted them to be. I see a danger in building relationships with students that have no long-term purpose. Dr. Lindsay challenged me to be a friend to young people with the purpose of leading them to maturity in Christ.

This concept reminds me of the statement made by the young missionary, Jim Elliott. I have this quote written in the flyleaf of my Bible, "Father, make me a crises man. Bring those I come into contact with to a decision. Let me not be a milepost on a single road. Make me a fork, that men must turn one way or the other on seeing Christ in me."[3] This is what being a leader of youth really means. We must build relationships that allow us to lead students to follow Christ.

So how do we go about developing meaningful relationships with students? I am still learning myself, but here are a few suggestions that I practice in my own ministry. I have watched these simple endeavors open doors and the hearts of students.

1. Get into their world. It's vital that we go onto their turf. It's important that we get off the church property and go to them. I have been challenged through the years to take at least one day a week and have lunch with some students on a high school campus. This gets me out of my office and into their world. It's amazing how many of them are shocked to see you walk into their lunch room.

2. **Take them with you.** I've also made it a habit of taking students with me to share Christ with the lost. You would be surprised how you can get to know a student while you're in the car driving to another student's home to share with them about the claims of Christ. You can find out all about them, about their families, and what is going on in their spiritual lives. I simply like to ask questions. "Hey, tell me about your family. Who are your brothers and sisters?" All of this can be done while you are allowing them to be a part of ministry to others.

3. **Go to their school activities.** I like to watch our students participate in sporting events and other school activities such as plays and concerts. Whether it's a Friday night football game, a track meet, a swim meet, a vocal performance, or something else, I like to watch students excel in the things they love to do. This opens the door for conversation and gives you another opportunity to affirm them. Because you show interest, it builds relationships. Students love to see significant adults come to their activities.

4. **Have them in your home.** I also like to have the teenagers visit in our home. Recently, we developed a program for our seniors, which included fellowship at my house. It was a joy to have forty or so twelfth graders in our home for fellowship. There was a teaching time, but the majority of the time was fellowship: eating, laughing, and just sharing. I believe we gained a lot of ground with those young people because they were in our home.

If we are serious about building relationships with our students, then we have to get into their world. I say it again—get off the sacred property, leave your office, leave the church building and go where they are living every day. This type of ministry is incredibly rewarding. Over the years, I have watched teens' lives changed through the godly influence of caring adult youth leaders.

I'll never forget listening to a student share his testimony at one of our events. I was so excited to hear what he had to say. At the time, this young man was a struggling high schooler about to graduate. He wanted to share about what had influenced him the most in his relationship with Jesus Christ. I was waiting for him to talk about some great camp, crusade, Sunday school lesson, or youth meeting that had changed his life. Tears ran down his cheeks as he talked about the time an adult leader called, picked him up, and took him out to get a hamburger.

There it was before my eyes, a living example of dynamic ministry in the life of a young person because a leader intentionally built a relationship. This young man was so impressed that the adult would be involved in his life. By the way, I later had the opportunity to perform the wedding of this young man and his beautiful bride who grew up in our church. He has gone on to live a very vibrant Christian life.

One of the blessings of being in student ministry for many years is seeing the long-term fruit of your ministry. Many times over, I have asked young adults who grew up in our church youth ministry this question: "What are the things that most impacted your life for Christ through the youth ministry?" It's amazing to me how the majority of them talk about relationships with godly leaders who cared about them. What a return on that investment.

As your student ministry grows, it is imperative that you pour your life into other adult youth workers who can multiply ministry. They will reach students you may never know. Some of the same practical steps can build relationships with other leaders. Have them in your home, meet them for lunch, and set up training times with them. Youth leadership retreats are a great tool for connecting in heart and spirit. As you disciple them in their spiritual disciplines, they will do the same with other teens. You will multiply your ministry if you build relationships with other adults who will carry on your passion for students.

So what are we going to do? Remember, youth calendars can be the busiest calendars on the planet. The planning and execution of concerts, camps, and events is important. But in the midst of all the planning for the crowds, make sure to develop a strategy to build a one-on-one relationship with students. The goal is to equip teens with the tools for personal growth and exporting of their faith. I believe those relationships will yield the greatest impact for the kingdom. The examples of Jesus and Paul create influence us to have lasting fruit from our years of student ministry.

Dr. Oscar Thompson was right. Outside of the obvious answers of Jesus and the Bible, the most important word relative to ministry is "relationships."

NOTES

1. Robert E. Coleman, *The Master Plan of Evangelism*, 2nd ed. (Grand Rapids, MI: Fleming H. Revel, 1993), 31.

2. Gary Dausey, ed., *The Youth Leaders' Sourcebook* (City: Zondervan, 1983), 51-61.

3. Elisabeth Elliot, *Shadow of the Almighty: The Life and Testament of Jim Elliot* (New York: Harper, 1958).

TEACHING OTHERS TO BE WHAT I ALREADY AM

Ric Garland

There you stand before a room full of students. You are fixed on the intimidating, deep, dark stares from their eyes. They are all looking at you, the leader. All of a sudden the concept of discipleship traverses from a cliché to a reality. You are confronted with the biblical mandate of "making disciples."

Unfortunately, discipleship is overused as a term but underused as a practice. We would like to believe that discipleship is the strategic success of the twenty-first century youth group, but often it is nothing more than a conversation topic. The goal is to move discipleship from dominating our conversations to penetrating our ministries. Helping teens connect the Word of God to their everyday lives and choices can be a reality. Training them to be godly in an ungodly society is more than a dream; it is a biblical necessity.

One of the challenges we have to overcome in this generation is the high tech-low touch paradigm. Culturally and generally, we have accelerated the pace of life and expanded the fountain of knowledge. Yet teens of this decade are often empty and untouched by an involved, caring adult.

Students have been equipped with enough resources to help them grow, or at least expand their knowledge, in any area they desire. Operationally, with the click of a mouse and a surf on the Net, they have any desired data. They have the technical tools and the resources, but what they really need is a youth leader who is committed to long-term discipleship to help them maneuver through the maze of life.

Transfer this thought from the pages of this book to the realm of your personal influence. Do you have students who often feel they've been "left alone" to blindly discover their own way in walking with Christ? If you are honest, then the answer is probably yes. There are teens within our own groups who lack the intervention of an adult leader's assistance in moving them from spiritual infancy to maturity in Christ, otherwise known as the path of discipleship.

When we bring this home personally, it sometimes creates questions or even panic. "Who me? Disciple someone? I can't do that. I don't think I'm qualified. Where would I start? What would I say? When would I find the time to disciple?" If these words reflect your thoughts, you are in good company because there are good and godly leaders all across this country who feel the same inadequacy. But the opportunity to make a difference hinges on one word, WILLINGNESS! You are reading this right now because you have a willingness to help, a willingness to invest your life in the life of another and, most importantly, a willingness to obey Christ's words: "Go therefore and make disciples of all the nations, baptizing them in the name of the Father and of the Son and of the Holy Spirit" (Matthew 28:19).

THE DEFINITION OF DISCIPLESHIP

What does *discipleship* mean? Discipleship is not about "me talk, you listen!" It's more of a "let's grow together" concept. Ultimately, we define *discipleship* as "teaching others to be what I already am." That does not mean that you are an authority on everything. In essence, it's not just telling someone else how to live, but it is showing them. It doesn't require perfection on your part, only that you are an example of a growing Christian. Paul said, "The things which you learned and received and heard and saw in me, these do, and the God of peace will be with you" (Philippians 4:9). It's a God-given responsibility that begins with one person demonstrating to another an intimate relationship with God. Practicing biblical discipleship is evidenced through a life that is contagious.

Discipleship in its purest sense is not just mentoring. "Mentoring" is a biblical concept but refers to teaching in a general sense. Your pastor mentors every Sunday morning when he preaches. Teachers mentor when they teach. Mentoring is a part of discipleship that is more personal, more specific. We can mentor others in sports, in cooking, or in any other skill. But discipleship, in the biblical sense, goes beyond instruction. It is influencing another person through your words and life so they can apply the Word of God to their everyday lives.

A strong element of discipleship is change—on the part of the discipler and the disciplee. Change can be viewed as a negative that puts us on edge. But discipleship is being willing to make changes and grow. The personal involvement in another's life is characterized by change as each sharpens the other's walk with Christ.

Philippians 1:9–10 says, "And this I pray, that your love may abound still more and more in knowledge and all discernment, that you may approve the things that are excellent, that you may be sincere and without offense till the day of Christ." Paul challenges us to be willing to change for the sake of excellence. As we disciple others, we must keep this goal before them as well.

Discipleship means knowing someone closely enough to help him or her grow spiritually. As we build our relationship, we then begin to discern how to move the person in the desired direction. The basis for change is your goal to guide another person to maturity under the working of the Holy Spirit. We instruct them in being conformed to the image of Christ and influence them to model the reality of each truth. We have the opportunity to see teens change, and even better, to help make Christ real and dynamic in their everyday lives.

Discipleship takes the abstract and gives it substance. Teens have moved from their concrete ways of thinking as a child to abstract thinking through adolescence. Therefore, it is characteristic for a teen to resist change and maybe even to develop a negative attitude. They may communicate frustration regarding their comprehension of the Word of God and defensively use a ploy such as "I just don't understand the Bible, and I cannot do this." We must guard them from allowing this thought pattern to become concrete, thus damaging their growth.

"Discipleship is about teaching one of 'God's own' to become a disciple of Christ".[1] Dr. J. Dwight Pentecost, in his book *Design for Discipleship*, states the following:

> One becomes a disciple in the biblical sense only when one is totally and completely committed to the person of Jesus Christ and His Word. It involves setting aside one's own will and one's own rights to his life and acknowledging that Jesus Christ has the right to be obeyed, the right to rule. A disciple is one who has a consuming passion for the person of Christ, whose heart is set upon the person of Christ, who has an unshakeable confidence in the Word of Christ and is completely committed to Christ in service and obedience.

This can be overwhelming unless we view it as a process of development. The concept stated by Dr. Pentecost is more easily accepted if one knows, "I have someone who cares about me, who is willing to walk alongside of me and teach me." On paper, Pentecost's quote is inspiring; lived out, it is both contagious and igniting.

Many teens (and adults) left on their own will choose to take the easy path of living like everyone else in the world. Given the enticements and lures of Satan, our adversary (1 Peter 5:8), this promotes a carnal mindset and lifestyle. There must be intentional intervention to help a teen establish a dynamic walk with Christ. A person is needed who, on a regular basis, encourages them to grow and stay strong in the things of God.

Discipleship presents open forums allowing the teen the

opportunity to ask difficult questions that haunt their thoughts and lives. These forums are provided by responsive, loving adults who help steer their untrained affections and concerns to biblical answers. You will not always have the answers. Discipleship is about being willing to help them find the answers in the only reliable source, the Word of God.

Before we go any further, let me reemphasize a major point. Biblical discipleship is the overflowing of your personal walk with Christ onto another. Therefore, the very basis of discipleship must be a vigorous personal walk with Christ on the part of the discipler. Many times this is the roadblock to discipleship; it is often the key to defining why discipleship is not occurring. There is a lack in the adult's disciplined walk and spiritual growth.

Where there is a void of daily learning and individual alertness to personal spiritual growth, there will be a hollowness of concern for another's growth. This creates a cavity of fear and paralyzes a drive or desire for discipleship. Yet Romans 15:13 speaks of an opposite response when it says, "Now may the God of hope fill you with all joy and peace in believing, that you may abound in hope by the power of the Holy Spirit."

What happens to you when you are "bumped," figuratively speaking, by another? Does the Word of God splash out of you? We are aware that "out of the abundance of the heart the mouth speaks," (Matthew 12:34); therefore, a discipler's heart is connected practically to the reality of what God is first doing in their own lives. Once that is established, there is no way to contain it.

One of the key truths to be considered by the discipler and shared with the disciplee is Romans 6:11, "Likewise you also, reckon yourselves to be dead indeed to sin, but alive to God in Christ Jesus our Lord." This vital verse is foundational in helping teens who are abstract thinkers to walk in the Spirit. A discipler has the privilege of taking this truth from an intangible concept and demonstrating it as solid truth.

Reckon in this verse also means "to consider." In other words, we should occupy ourselves with the thought, the *truth*, that we are "dead" to sin; sinful actions and thoughts should no longer have an active part in our lives because of Christ's conquering spirit. Thus, you have a word picture to illustrate that we are powerless to live the "Christian life" on our own. The completing ingredient is the realization that I am "alive" in Christ: He wants to live His life through me. As we disciple, we make connections between the Word of God and the practical daily life.

But as with all truth we are imparting, it must first be considered and appropriated by the discipler. Again we are not talking about perfection; we are talking about maturing in our faith. We have a responsibility to practice what we preach. We are not just passing along some "new" revelation we have discovered; we are transferring truth through the vehicle of our lives. Approaching discipleship with this mindset will protect us from placing ourselves on a pedestal because it points others to the Savior, who is working in us and empowering us. Biblical discipleship is look and live, looking to Jesus and following His example.

It all begins with the foundation of the Word of God but manifests itself in a teen's daily life. Share with a teen those things that add value to life. For example, when they personally discover the influence they can have by living out biblical principles, it will produce an excitement and energy in their Christian lives. As they walk the halls of their school, attend parties or even youth group, they can communicate the power of God in their lives. Their lives will become a walking billboard to a lost world about the victory available in Christ.

I have laid the foundation or principle, but now we need to consider some practical steps. Even though the foundation has been laid—and perhaps some goal-setting accomplished—without the "how-tos," the message may get lost in the whirlwind of a teen's life. A discipler seals the concept by interlinking the disciplee's heart with the "how-tos" of personally living out truth.

THE DIRECTION OF DISCIPLESHIP

The "hows" are the strategy for discipleship. As disciplers, we have chosen to be involved in another's life. Therefore, we become a student of the teen, giving focused attention. We want to understand the heartbeat, pressures, and struggles he faces. Guided by the Holy Spirit, we will become aware of the "strongholds" of the one we disciple. We do not need to make this more complicated than it is. Simply asking questions prompted by the Holy Spirit will take us past shallowness to the issues of the heart.

We all have strongholds in our lives, sins that seem to hold us captive. Yet Christ came to set the captive free—to set us free so we can live in freedom. Galatians 5:1 says, "Stand fast therefore in the liberty by which Christ has made us free, and do not be entangled again with a yoke of bondage." Obedience brings peace. Therefore, you must help the ones you disciple to know the steps of obedience that will gain freedom, life, and peace in their lives (Romans 8:6). Biblical discipleship is application of the Word.

Our Savior was the master of this principle. He moved freely from compassion to application and instruction (Luke 5:12–14). A poignant example is Christ's interaction with a man having leprosy. Jesus Christ was moved with compassion. He then reached out and healed the man, taught this man who He was, and instructed him clearly on the next steps to take. Our Savior did the equivalent with the woman at the well. Having compassion for her, He instructed her regarding the living water as well as her next steps (John 4:1–26). Please note: the man with leprosy was instructed what not to do, "See that you tell no one; but go your way, show yourself to the priest . . ." In contrast, the Samarian woman was told what to do, "Worship in spirit and truth."

And so it must be for us: compassion followed by teaching and stabilized by steps of application. Application of Scripture must be apparent and understandable to include both the negatives and the positives. It is the principle of put off and put on: "The night is far spent, the day is at hand. Therefore let us cast off the works of darkness, and let us put on the armor of light" (Romans 13:12). "All Scripture . . . is profitable" (2 Timothy 3:16), not only to edify and encourage, but also to reproof and correct in order to help one conform to God's will and purpose. Discipleship must include steps of application, which are solid and focused to connect Scripture with a teen's life.

The person you are discipling may struggle with the personal application of the truths he or she has learned. Our goal is to know this person intimately enough to help knit truths from Scripture into moment-by-moment life. Motivate the heart to practically live out truth and walk in the light. Remember, follow-up will be critical. Never shy away from keeping a disciple accountable. Remember it is not what you "expect" that will come to fruition, but what you "inspect." Ask him to report to you with the results of application.

THE DECISION OF DISCIPLESHIP

Discipleship is exciting, personal, and practical. Exciting people excite other people. "Brethren, join in following my example . . ." (Philippians 3:17). As a discipler, examine your heart and settle this question, "Does the Word of God excite me?" If so, you have the opportunity to pass that on to another. Remember, effective discipleship does not take place from a distance; it is up close and personal. Discipleship will be practical as we live out what God is doing in our lives and others catch the enthusiasm of our lives.

A holy life is a life that will affect others. Paul addresses this when he says, "You are witnesses, and God also, how devoutly and justly and blamelessly we behaved ourselves among you who believe" (1 Thessalonians 2:10). As disciplers, we live in the "fish bowl" because we are being watched. Striving to live without hypocrisy and being careful in our actions becomes a lifestyle. We all behave differently when we know we're being watched, and, as a result, it will sharpen us!

In 1 Thessalonians 2:4, we are challenged: "But as we have been approved by God to be entrusted with the gospel, even so we speak, not as pleasing men, but God who tests our hearts." Notice the three parts of this verse. First, "we were allowed of God." Discipleship is an awesome responsibility entrusted to us by God.

Second, "so we speak." As disciplers we have a responsibility to speak to the ones we are discipling concerning their spiritual growth. This means that we lovingly speak the truth as Ephesians 4:15 admonishes. Difficult issues will arise in the discipleship process, and we must be committed to addressing them with truth even when it is uncomfortable. Edifying, comforting, and correcting are all a part of the discipleship process. "As you know how we exhorted, and comforted, and charged every one of you, as a father *does* his own children" (1 Thessalonians 2:11). As a "father" who is often a bottom-line type of person, we must seek to get to the bottom line and speak honestly.

Third, Paul says "not as pleasing men, but God." All that we say and do as disciplers is guided by our motive to solely please God. Biblical discipleship is an incredible responsibility but is extremely rewarding.

Discipleship requires a commitment of your heart to another person. Paul expresses this so well when he says, "So, affectionately longing for you, we were well pleased to impart to you not only the gospel of God, but also our own lives, because you had become dear to us (1 Thessalonians 2:8). You must have a heart for the one you disciple, showing them esteem and giving care.

As disciplers, we want to settle on the goal for the individual God has entrusted to us. We will be "out of our comfort zone" at times as we embark on this spiritual journey. But remembering and focusing on the ultimate goal will energize and encourage us. "So that He may establish your hearts blameless in holiness before our God and Father at the coming of our Lord Jesus Christ with all His saints" (1 Thessalonians 3:13).

"For what is our hope, or joy, or crown of rejoicing? Is it

not even you in the presence of our Lord Jesus Christ at His coming? For you are our glory and joy (1 Thessalonians 2:19–20). What an incredible thought. Paul had the right perspective of discipleship. He kept the "big picture," realizing that his investment in the lives of people was eternal. So what about you? Are you ready to make the decision to disciple? Why not find someone today to pour your life into?

NOTE

1. J. Dwight Pentecost, *Design for Discipleship: Discovering God's Blueprint for the Christian Life* (Grand Rapids, MI: Kregel Publications, 1996), pp. 14-15.

BUILDING A GREAT STUDENT MINISTRY

Ben Brown

Can you imagine simply announcing a Christian service opportunity and having more students respond than you could accommodate? Or how about getting them to participate in community service during their spring break? This sounds great, but is it realistic? Can this be the norm and not the exception in our youth ministries?

For the sake of illustration, I am using a personal example that answers that question positively. I have to admit: at Pleasant View Bible Church where I serve, we have had an incredible experience in this area of ministry. I am not using this as the *ex-officio* model; I am just sharing it by way of encouragement.

At our church, planning an event like a Community Service Day or an Evangelistic Car Wash will bring the students out in mass numbers. Our volunteer rosters for music and children's ministries are filled with students' names. Often our teens outnumber the people they are ministering to at the nursing homes or rescue missions. On our annual spring break missions trip to inner-city Chicago, students give up their school vacations to tutor children during the school day at an inner-city elementary school and to spend their evenings helping with a children's ministry.

I know what you're thinking—"That's not natural!" Exactly right, and while we view this as a blessing from God, at the same time I have to admit there are some strategic reasons for what we are experiencing. I hope you are asking, "How can God use my youth ministry team at our church to motivate students to serve the Lord?" That is the question I want to answer in this chapter by laying the biblical foundation for service to Christ.

A PORTRAIT OF A SERVANT

Before we can effectively motivate students to be biblical servants, we need to establish a model for them. "Servant" in our English New Testament usually represents the Greek word that literally means "a bondservant." Bondservants were the property of the person who purchased them. Their lives were not at their own disposal. Bought to serve their master's needs, bondservants were at his beck and call every moment. Their sole business was to do what they were told.

Like the bondslaves in the times of the New Testament, we have been purchased by Christ and are thereby responsible to use our bodies to honor Him (1 Corinthians 6:19–20).

We are obligated to do as the Master who bought us commands, expecting no special treatment for doing what is expected of us (Luke 17:7–10).

Another of the Greek words that is translated "servant" literally means "under rower" (1 Corinthians 4:1). It refers to those in the belly of the ship who would row the boat under the direction of a seaman.

Likewise, as Christ's servants, we are subordinate to Him. We are responsible to live under our Lord's direction.

What does Christ expect His bondservants to do? He directs us to serve others for His sake (2 Corinthians 4:5). Christ made us free from slavery (to sin) and bondage (to a legalistic system) not so that we can do whatever we want, but so that we can serve one another (Galatians 5:13). We serve our Master by becoming servants of our fellow bondservants in Christ.

When we serve others as Christ would have us to serve, what things characterize our service? True service for Christ welcomes all opportunities to serve. It makes no difference if an opportunity is large or small. It rests contented in obscurity, unconcerned about whether it receives external reward or human applause. It does not need to calculate its results or display its achievements. The divine nod of approval is sufficient.

True service for Christ does not expect anything in return. It does not choose whom to serve; it serves indiscriminately and without conditions. It can serve enemies as freely as friends. It does every task with the same dedication, no matter if its object is lovely or ugly, high and powerful, or low and defenseless. True service for Christ will stoop to meet the needs of others even if others consider such acts undignified.

True service for Christ is not an event, but a lifestyle choice. It does not function only when a specific service is being performed, but it springs spontaneously wherever a need presents itself. It does not wait for the need to come to it; it searches out opportunities to help others.[1]

The best portrait of what a servant looks like is the life our Lord Jesus Christ; He is our supreme example:

> For even the Son of Man did not come to be served, but to serve, and to give His life a ransom for many (Mark 10:45).

> Now before the Feast of the Passover, when Jesus knew that His hour had come that He should depart from this world to the Father, having loved His own who were in the world, He loved them to the end. And supper being ended, the devil having already put it into the heart of Judas Iscariot, Simon's *son*, to betray Him, Jesus, knowing that the Father had given all things into His hands, and that He had come from God and was going to God, rose from supper and laid aside His garments, took a towel and girded Himself. After that, He poured water into a basin and began to wash the disciples' feet, and to wipe *them* with the towel with which He was girded. If I then, *your* Lord and Teacher, have washed your feet, you also ought to wash one another's

feet. For I have given you an example, that you should do as I have done to you (John 13:1–5; 14–15).

For you know the grace of our Lord Jesus Christ, that though He was rich, yet for your sakes He became poor, that you through His poverty might become rich (2 Corinthians 8:9).

Let this mind be in you which was also in Christ Jesus, who, being in the form of God, did not consider it robbery to be equal with God, but made Himself of no reputation, taking the form of a bondservant, *and* coming in the likeness of men. And being found in appearance as a man, He humbled Himself and became obedient to *the point of* death, even the death of the cross (Philippians 2:5–8).

By this we know love, because He laid down His life for us. And we also ought to lay down *our* lives for the brethren (1 John 3:16).

Though Christ is God, He made himself nothing and took on the very nature of a servant. Though Christ was rich, for our sakes He became poor. Christlike service helps provide for the needs of others, loving them in actions and in truth (1 John 3:17–18). It considers the needs and interests of others ahead of its own (Romans 12:10; Philippians 2:3–4).

GOD'S MOTIVATORS WORK BEST!

The biblical portrait of a servant contrasts the way the world encourages us to live. In the world, personal rights are considered a higher priority than one's responsibility to others. When deciding on an action, the first questions we are encouraged to ask are, "What's in it for me?" and "What do I have to give up?" In this atmosphere, how can we effectively motivate students to a life of sacrificial, selfless service? The best place to begin is to teach the motivations God gives for ministry.

God motivates us to surrender our lives to Him by His mercy for us (Romans 12:1). Given all that God mercifully did to provide us with the gift of salvation, how could we do anything less than present ourselves to Him as living sacrifices, allowing Him to use us however He pleases? The only logical act of worship that appropriately corresponds to what God has done is to commit, "I want God's will in my life more than anything else." Only total dedication of our lives to God is an appropriate response to His mercy.

Christ's love for us compels us to live as selfless servants (2 Corinthians 5:15–16). Paul's reflection on Christ's death in payment of the penalty for his sins compelled him to ministry. We could say that Paul was so constrained by the love of Christ that it hemmed him in on all sides, giving him no choice but to go in one direction—to selflessly minister the gospel. Christ did not die on the cross so that we can strive after our selfish pursuits. Christ died, intending that we who receive new life in Him will live for Him.

Christ's judgment and His promised rewards motivate us to serve Him (2 Corinthians 5:9–10). Understanding he would stand before Christ to be judged and held accountable for his life, the apostle Paul made it his goal to please Him. As we anticipate Christ's judgment seat as believers, there are five points Paul makes in 2 Corinthians 5:10 that we need to keep in mind. First, we all must face Christ's judgment. While a Christian may or may not live a life of service for Christ, avoiding judgment is not an option. No one will be exempt from standing before the Lord.

Second, each individual will be judged separately. Notice how Paul moves from "we" to "each one." We will each have to give a personal account for what we have done. It is our tendency to compare what we do with what others do. Since what others do is not the standard by which Christ will judge us, and since it is unwise to compare ourselves with others (2 Corinthians 10:12), we should concentrate on being faithful in our own works and not concern ourselves with what others are doing.

Third, we will be judged for the works we have done. The believers' judgment examines our practice, not our position. Our position in Christ has already been determined by the time we arrive at the judgment seat of Christ. If we are at this judgment, we are there because we are saved. The unsaved are judged separately at the Great White Throne Judgment (Revelation 20:11–15).

Fourth, the believer will "appear" at the time of the Judgment Seat of Christ. This does not mean that believers will "show up on their day in court." Rather, we will "be manifested." Our lives will be turned inside out, and all we have done will be laid bare before the Lord to see and judge.[2]

Fifth, the result of the judgment seat of Christ is that our works will be shown to be either good or bad. Christ will judge us based on the quality of our works. Good, quality works will bring us reward. Bad or useless works will result in losing reward (See 1 Corinthians 3:10–15).

What makes a work good or bad? It is clear from 1 Corinthians 4:1–2 that a significant factor in Christ's determination as to whether or not we receive rewards is our faithfulness as stewards of what He entrusts us to do in His service. Another key factor for determining how Christ will judge us is our motivation (1 Corinthians 4:5). Self-serving acts of ministry will not be rewarded.

What rewards can we expect to receive for faithful service? The Bible specifically talks about five rewards. There is a crown of life for those who faithfully endure trials (James 1:12), an imperishable crown for those who live a disciplined life of self-denial (1 Corinthians 9:25), a crown of glory for those who faithfully shepherd the flock (1 Peter 5:4), a crown of righteousness for those who love Christ's appearing (2 Timothy 4:8), and a crown of rejoicing for those who faithfully witness (1 Thessalonians 2:19).

Some say that we shouldn't motivate others to serve by visualizing the rewards God will give for faithfulness. After all, what we do in ministry should be done out of love for God and concern for His glory, not so that we will receive rewards. The problem with this reasoning is that it ignores how God clearly uses rewards as motivators for faithful service in His Word. God uses rewards to prompt us to give our lives to things that matter for eternity rather than squandering them on temporal things.

Our examples motivate students to serve. While God's motivations work best, He can and will use our example to motivate students to serve. The fact God uses human examples is evident from Paul's statement in 1 Corinthians 11:1—Imitate me, just as I also *imitate* Christ.

Motivate students to serve by modeling selfless humility. Students encounter a self-centered world that blasts out its message at every turn. They click on their televisions and what do they hear? "Have it *your* way" and "Everything *you* need, nothing you don't."

The world tells students, "We have to look out for Number One. Whatever we need to do to advance ourselves, we should do." God's Word teaches students, "Let nothing be done through selfish ambition or conceit, but in lowliness of mind let each esteem others better than himself. Let each of you look out not only for his own interests, but also for the interests of others" (Philippians 2:3–4). The world says, "First one to the top wins," but the Word says the first one to the servant's towel wins (see Mark 10:42–45). The world promotes striving after the limelight and looking for the applause of men; whereas, servants of Christ maintain a low profile, focused on pleasing God, not men (Galatians 1:10).

How can we help students to live a life of humble, selfless service instead of living to promote themselves? We, like Paul, need to serve as examples of a life spent in service to others. Paul told the church in Corinth, "And I will very gladly spend and be spent for your souls; though the more abundantly I love you, the less I am loved" (2 Corinthians 12:15). On behalf of the Philippian church, Paul viewed himself as "being poured out as a drink offering" (Philippians 2:17).

Practically speaking, we need to evaluate honestly how we are doing at modeling selfless service. When involved in a pickup game of basketball or volleyball with our students, are we focused on serving them by helping them to enjoy a good time together and making sure everyone is included, or are we more concerned about winning the game and showing off our athletic skills? When we get a call in the middle of the night from a student with a desperate need, do we communicate that we are glad to serve even then, or do we act frustrated from having to get out of bed at that hour? When our schedule is interrupted by an unexpected appointment, do we act frustrated that our plans will have to be rearranged, or do we show that we view the "interruption" not as an inconvenience but as a divine appointment to serve? When it comes to our daily routine, are we putting in our time, or are we pouring out our lives?

Motivate students to serve by modeling love in ministry. Students live in a world plagued by the philosophy of postmodernism that preaches, "There are no absolutes: what is true for one person is not necessarily true for another." In this culture, how can we convince students that the message of the Bible is absolute truth? How can we convince them of the absolute truth that the best way to live is to consider Jesus first, others second, and one's self last?

It is easy for some students to discount what we teach them about biblical service. A common response postmodern "doubters" will give to instruction on the subject is, "That is good for you, but I have a different way that is good for me. Don't judge me for what I think is true, and I won't judge you." While some students might easily be able to discount what we say, it is much more difficult for them to ignore the truth we share when it is supported by our love. When our exhortation for students to serve the Lord is accompanied by the love God produces in us for others, students will be much more likely to listen to the truth we share. The old adage is still true: "Students don't care how much we know until they know how much we care." Like Paul, we need to love others so much that we delight to share with them not only the gospel but also our lives, because they have become so dear to us (1 Thessalonians 2:8).

Motivate students to serve by modeling dependence on God's power. One of the most significant discouragements to serving the Lord is when we attempt a ministry and experience miserable failure. When encouraged to serve again, we say things like, "I tried that, but I fell on my face." Sometimes, the problem is that we need to be encouraged to try a different area of ministry that better suits how the Lord has prepared us for service. More often than we would like to admit, our problem is a lack of dependence on God. When we try to serve in the flesh, we fail. When we try to serve God without His power by gritting our teeth and putting forth our best effort, the results do not look pretty.

It is not helpful when we try to motivate students to service by asking them, "What are we going to do to make a difference for the Lord?" A question like this can so easily mislead students into thinking that to serve the Lord effectively they need to work harder to make something happen. A more motivating question is, "What great things can we trust God to do in and through us in His service?" This question helps students to focus on trusting God to work in and through them as they serve rather than trying to serve God in the flesh.

The apostle Paul was a great example of service because He depended on Christ's power. Paul wrote in Colossians 1:28–29: "Him we preach, warning every man and teaching every man in all wisdom, that we may present every man perfect in Christ Jesus. To this end I also labor, striving according to His working which works in me mightily." When Paul suffered incredible hardship in ministry, he did not lament his weaknesses. Instead, he understood that he was but a jar of clay in the hands of his master and that his frailty showed the "all-surpassing power [for ministry of the gospel] is from God and not from us" (2 Corinthians 4:7 NIV). When Paul's request for the re-moval of the thorn in the flesh was denied, Paul responded to Christ's answer, "Therefore most gladly I will rather boast in my infirmities, that the power of Christ may rest upon me. Therefore I take pleasure in infirmities, in reproaches, in needs, in persecutions, in distresses, for Christ's sake. For when I am weak, then I am strong" (2 Corinthians 12:9b–10). We need to be vigilant in our reminders to students that apart from Christ's power working in and through them, they can do nothing. Jesus states in John 15:5, "I am the vine, you are the branches. He who abides in Me, and I in him, bears much fruit; for without Me you can do nothing." A branch can do nothing on its own apart from the vine. For a branch to bear fruit, it must abide in the vine, drawing from it the sustenance or nour-ishment needed for fruit production. Likewise, for us to bear fruit in our service for Christ, we must abide in Him, drawing from Him the sustenance we need for fruitful service.

We abide in Christ when we spend time in communion with Him, reading His communication to us in the Word, and communicating back to Him by our prayers for His will to be accomplished. Only as we depend on Christ and the work of the Holy Spirit will our lives produce the fruits of service that please God (Galatians 5:16, 22–23). Until we realize we can do nothing without Christ, we will accomplish nothing for Him by our acts of service, no matter how hard we try.

THE TIME FOR STUDENTS TO SERVE THE LORD IS NOW!

"Students are the church of tomorrow!" What thought comes to mind when this statement is made? Our response should be, "No, students are not just the church of tomorrow, they are a vital part of the church today!" We do not train students so they can serve later as adults. We equip students to serve God right now.

It's extremely difficult to motivate students to serve the

Lord if they remain unconvinced that ministry is their present responsibility. Ephesians 4:11–12 makes it clear that ministry is for all believers, not just the church's adult leaders. The work of the church's leadership is not to do all the work themselves, but to equip the saints for the work of the ministry, so that the body of Christ might be built up. Many have the mistaken idea that Christian service is what pastors and youth pastors are paid to do. Many youth leaders volunteer and are not paid, but just the same, the people of the church expect them to do all the work of youth ministry. Church leaders, paid or volunteer, are given to the church not to do all the work for the church, but to prepare its people to do the ministry themselves.

Let's think about our own patterns as youth leaders. How much of our time is spent equipping and training others? As we think about our key night for student ministries, how much do we involve students in what is going on? In the upcoming calendar, how many events and lessons do we have planned that are designed to equip students to serve the Lord? Are students involved in other church ministries outside of youth group? If we really believe students are a part of today's church, we will show it by how we involve them in service to the body of Christ. When students graduate from high school, will they leave our churches because they never felt a part of their ministries, or will they be excited to continue ministering with us because our churches believe God uses young people?

EVERY STUDENT HAS A PURPOSE; EVERY STUDENT NEEDS TO SERVE

Students are looking for a sense of purpose in life. Their world offers little that is really worth living for. As youth leaders, we have an incredible opportunity to be used to "turn students on" to purpose—God's purpose! Young people need to understand that every believer is created in Christ to do good works (Ephesians 2:10). Christian students are God's workmanship. They were created in Christ for the purpose of doing the good works that He, long ago, prepared for them to do. We could say that students have an eternally designed job description. Talk about an incredible purpose for them to get excited about!

Our expectations of students need to be raised. The bar is set too low if we are content that only a modest percentage of students in our youth ministry are involved in regular Christian service. Our expectation should be that every one of our students be involved in Christian service. Not one believer can legitimately say that God does not have an important ministry for him or her to do. Not one! How can we be so dogmatic on this point? Because we know that every believer is given a spiritual gift that he or she is responsible to use faithfully to serve the body of Christ (1 Corinthians 12:7; 1 Peter 4:10). The apostle Peter calls us "good stewards of the manifold grace of God." Stewards were household managers who had no wealth of their own, but distributed their master's wealth according to his will and direction. In the same way, students are stewards of the spiritual gifts God has given them. They are responsible to use these gifts according to their Master's will and direction.

STUDENTS NEED OUR ENCOURAGEMENT!

When asked who had the greatest influence in our lives in terms of motivating us to serve God, who do we immediately think of? We remember the people who were confident God was going to use us in His work even though we didn't see it at the time. Their confidence led us to trust God to use us in His service.

Now it is our turn to encourage young people. When a student serves Christ's body in such a way that it is obvious that "God did that," we need to send an e-mail, make a phone call, or put our arm around his or her shoulder to affirm God's work. Remember what such affirmation did in our lives when we received it as young people? Now, let's go and do likewise.

Let's faithfully remind students of Christ's example and God's motivation for service. Let's model what a biblical servant looks like. Most importantly, let's depend on God's power, because the production of servants doesn't come naturally. A selfless servant is a supernatural product.

NOTES

1. Richard J. Foster, *Celebration of Discipline: The Path to Spiritual Growth* (San Francisco: Harper Collins Publishers, 1988), 128–130.

2. Robert Gromacki, *Stand Firm in the Faith: An Exposition of 2 Chronicles* (The Woodlands, TX: Kress Christian Publications, 2002), 83–85.

CAN A GIRL DO THAT?

Dr. Cheryl Fawcett

PERSONAL PERSPECTIVES

What a privilege to author this chapter! By the grace of God, I have enjoyed over thirty years in youth ministry as a woman—in the local church both as a paid staff member and as a volunteer. In God's providence, I have served and observed youth ministry firsthand in churches in Maryland, Pennsylvania, New York, Illinois, Ohio, and California. Over the last ten years, God has also allowed me to be involved in short-term youth ministry in England, Romania, Portugal, Alaska, and South Africa.

I have served in both rural and suburban churches. For twenty years, I played a support role in a teen leadership conference that fortified youth to serve God more fully in their churches, schools, and homes. It has been my privilege to equip and empower youth pastors, women in youth ministry, and youth volunteers at the college level for over twenty years. I have been respected, honored, ignored, and ridiculed.

I am completely satisfied with the role that God has given me as a single woman in youth ministry. I have no regrets! I am weary of reading articles about the glass ceiling that women face as they seek to serve. I am glad to report that you don't have to choose between biblical theology or practice as a woman in youth work. You don't have to serve in a theologically liberal church as a woman pastor to minister to youth effectively. You can be true to the dictates of Scripture and have a very significant ministry with youth whether they are male or female.

CURRENT GLOBAL NUMERICAL REALITIES

At the present time in world history, the continent of Africa contains nearly 75 percent of the population below age twenty. In most of South America, the population boasts 50 percent below the age of twenty, and in many places as high as 75 percent. There are as many youth in India as the entire population of the United States. In my estimation, there has never been a more opportune time in the history of the world to be alive, to serve God, and to be a Christian woman in youth ministry.

FAQS

I am frequently asked to lecture on the topic of women in youth ministry. I often begin those sessions by having students answer the following questions. Name three observations that you have about women doing youth ministry. List two potential benefits for involving women on the ministry team. Finally, write one question that you have regarding women serving with youth. Many observe that women are a necessary aspect of complete ministry to youth. Many notice the propensity of women toward carrying out the details of ministry. Nearly all acknowledge the role women play in modeling, teaching, and living the Christian life for both genders of youth.

Joseph Murray shares the sentiment that I have found to be true as a servant of Jesus Christ:

The more you do, the more you'll be asked to do.
That's the blessed penalty of willingness.
The more you do, the more you'll be able to do.
That's the blessed law of effort.
The more you do, the more it means to you.
That is the blessed promise of reward in the Master's service!

BIBLICAL MANDATES

Let's begin with a survey of biblical gender roles from Genesis through the New Testament era. Who has God chosen for leadership in ministry, and what roles did those individuals play?

So let's begin at the beginning. When God created Adam and Eve, He created them to be equal in value, equal in essence, and equal in mandate. Genesis 1:26–28 puts it,

> Then God said, "Let Us make man in Our image, according to Our likeness; let them have dominion over the fish of the sea, over the birds of the air, and over the cattle, over all the earth and over every creeping thing that creeps on the earth." So God created man in His *own* image; in the image of God He created him; male and female He created them. Then God blessed them, and God said to them, "Be fruitful and multiply; fill the earth and subdue it; have dominion over the fish of the sea, over the birds of the air, and over every living thing that moves on the earth.

Both Adam and Eve were needed to fulfill the divine directive to be fruitful and multiply and fill the earth. Man alone could not complete the task—and woman alone was likewise ill-equipped to complete the directive. God designed man and woman with an innate reliance on each other. Together in harmony, they could accomplish God's agenda. God specifically created Eve to complement or complete Adam (Genesis 2:18). She was not a weaker individual, easily prey to temptation, and thus not to be trusted. Instead, she was made to correspond to Adam in every way, making up what *he lacked*. She was his divine completion! Being a helper is not a negative role; God repeatedly calls Himself the helper of Israel, seventeen times in the Old Testament.[1]

That divine blessedness did not last very long before Satan was able to tempt Eve and Adam into sinful disobedience against God. Their sin led to brokenness (Genesis 3:16–19) and separation from God and the perfect fellowship they were meant to have with Him. Their desire to dominate each other was one of the consequences of their sin. Another consequence was the intense desire to exploit each other rather than work together in harmony (Genesis 4:7). From that day until this, sin has caused strife and conflict in relationships between man and woman. That conflict influences the relationships that men and women have in many arenas, including ministry roles. Like other effects of the curse, Christians need to fight off the desire to dominate the other gender while abandoning the divinely given tasks for their own gender.

PATRIARCHAL PATTERN OF LEADERSHIP

The patterns of the Old and New Testaments regarding primary spiritual leadership are remarkably consistent. God selected a series of male leaders to watch over the chosen nation Israel. The patriarchal leadership pattern began with Adam, who was held responsible for the sin committed by himself and his mate (Romans 5:12). Noah and his three sons were chosen to build a life-saving vehicle to preserve humanity from total destruction because of unabated sin (Genesis 6:13–14). Abram, Isaac, Jacob, and Joseph led God's chosen people. God selected Moses as the national leader when He was ready to deliver Israel from slavery. Aaron was God's choice for spiritual leader of the nation, and through Aaron's descendants, the Levites, male leaders performed priestly functions for hundreds of years.[2] For most of Israel's kingdom years, kings were chosen to lead God's people. All of the judges were male except for Deborah. God's selected male leaders included Jonah, Isaiah, Jeremiah, Ezekiel, Daniel, and others who performed the majority of the prophetic function.

There are some prophetesses chronicled in the history of Israel. Each were unique women of high moral character that God used—Miriam led a parade of jubilant women following the Red Sea crossing (Exodus 15), Deborah judged Israel in a time of great national oppression, and Huldah delivered God's message of coming judgment. While women were present, and provided occasional leadership, they did not consistently serve in the primary leadership role.

NEW TESTAMENT PATTERN OF LEADERSHIP

The New Testament pattern of leadership continues in a similar vein with Jesus' selection of all male disciples. Women were significant in the ministry of Jesus, but they were not the primary leaders (Luke 8:1–3). When the early church selected its first deacons, all were *men* of good reputation (Acts 6:1–6). Women are named in the early church as present (Acts 1:14) and involved but never in the primary leadership role. Apostles were those men who had seen Jesus and would later write the books and letters that would become authoritative for the church. Paul instructs Timothy in his selection of church leaders in Ephesus, explaining that they must be the husband of one wife to be pastors of local congregations (1 Timothy 3).

Women were present and recorded as serving, but women are never listed as the pastors of any congregation. Priscilla (multiple references, 2 Timothy 4), Lydia (Acts 16), Dorcas (Acts 9), Pheobe (Romans 16:1), Euodia and Syntyche (Philippians 4), Lois and Eunice (2 Timothy 1) are all named as active and influential in the early church. Paul frequently names women coworkers in the work of the church. Apphia is listed in his short letter to his friend Philemon who has a church meeting in his home (Philemon 2). Some believe that Apphia was Philemon's wife.

So were women of little value in the ministry of spreading the gospel? Was their role so diminished as to be of little use? No. As the infant church strove to establish itself, Paul wrote to the believers in Galatia, reminding them and us that the differences of race, gender, and economics should not cause any group to be of no import. He says plainly in Galatians 3:28 that

"There is neither Jew nor Greek, there is neither slave nor free, there is neither male nor female; for you are all one in Christ Jesus." In the functioning of the work of God, both genders are needed. Men are to take the primary leadership as women are fully engaged to complete the supporting roles.

PAULINE BOUNDARIES

It is plain to see from 2 Corinthians 5:17–20 that both men and women are redeemed in the same way—through the blood of Jesus Christ, the only sacrifice for sin. Likewise, both genders are commissioned to be ambassadors for Christ to a lost world. Second Corinthians 12, Ephesians 4, and Romans 12 each list areas of spiritual giftedness given to the redeemed for use in building the church of Christ. The gifts are not divided by gender. I believe, for instance, that I have been given the gift of pastor/teacher. My tendency is toward shepherding youth—that's pastoring. And teaching is a matter that I do without even thinking—God made me a teacher!

So, with all of this freedom are there any biblical limitations to what women can do in the church? Yes, there are boundaries, which Paul carefully lays out. In 1 Corinthians 11, the command is clearly given that women should pray and prophesy when the church gathers for worship and instruction. Paul also instructed women to display a proper sign of respect and submission—which in the first century was a head covering.

Again Paul has positive affirmations for the involvement of women in the early church when in 1 Timothy 2, he commands that the women learn—a clear violation of the cultural norms of that day when women were not admitted to formal teaching venues. In both 1 Corinthians 14:34 and 1 Timothy 2:11, women are instructed to worship in quietness (silence is not the most accurate translation of the Greek word used)—and if they have questions, to ask them at home of their husbands. Keep in mind that the seating in the early church was men in the front and women in the back—so to ask a question of your husband you must interrupt the service to get his attention. Rather, Paul encourages women to learn—to ask questions— but not to do so during the corporate worship.

So are all women to be in submission to all men? The instructions given by Paul are in the context of corporate worship and focused on husbands and their wives. The first congregations to read this letter from Paul were in the large seaport of Ephesus known for its false worship of the goddess Diana. Many perversions of worship were commonly practiced there to satisfy Diana, including the prostitution of women. In 1 Timothy 2, Paul gives specific instructions for the men regarding their prayer practices and the women regarding their apparel, hairstyles, and jewelry choices. Women are enjoined to dress "modestly, with decency and propriety," focusing on the inward matters of the heart not just the outward visible matters (vv. 9–10 NIV).

Paul goes on to address the proper attitudes for women in worship such as quietness and submission, rather than the screaming outbursts common in their neighbors' goddess worship. His desire was for wives to place themselves willingly under the authority of the church leadership and to exercise self-control.

The most troubling and hotly debated topic is the next section, in which Paul says women are not to teach or to have authority over a man. Numerous books have been written, giving a variety of interpretations. I will share my perspectives, but you need to search the Scriptures for yourself and come to your own conclusions.

There are several distinct words used in the New Testament that are all translated "teach" in English. Two Greek words dominate the New Testament's use of "teach," *didasko* and *katecheo*. *Didasko* is used frequently in the gospels and Acts and infrequently in the epistles. The kind of teaching that Jesus did was *didasko*. The apostles did *didasko*-style teaching. *Didasko* is an ongoing activity where one party helps another to learn. Only Luke and Paul use *katecheo*, and it is found later in the canon. It is rarely used in the Gospels. *Katecheo* means "to sound down, in place or time, into the ears of another." Actors on a stage are sounding down their lines to the ears of the audience. What is intended is that the script is already set, so now it is used to indoctrinate or catechize. So which kind of teaching does Paul forbid women from doing? *Didasko*? *Katecheo*?

Paul tells the women in Ephesus—many of whom were first-generation converts who had not been taught Scriptures and were indoctrinated in the pagan practices of goddess worship—not to *didasko*. It makes sense that they were not to be the authoritative congregational teacher. Paul is arguing for the women not to hold the office of congregational teacher. But at the end of his argument, Paul brings to witness the design of creation for the directives included here, which plainly reminds us that the restrictions were not meant for Ephesus and the first century alone but also for all who desire to minister within God's designed framework.

A quote from John McArthur's NKJV Study Bible is enlightening: "Women are not to be the public teachers when the church assembles, but neither are they to be shut out of the learning process. The form of the Greek verb . . . is an imperative. Paul is commanding women to be taught in the church, which was a novel concept. Since neither first century Judaism nor Greek culture held women in high esteem."[3]

Now, what do we make of the phrase "to have authority?" Again there are entire books written on this matter. Having studied myriads of them, I will share my conclusion. The King James Version translates it to "usurp authority," while the New American Standard Bible has "to exercise authority," and the New International Version says "have authority." The word used is very rare, not used anywhere else in Scripture and not used very often in the literature written at the same time as the letter of 1 Timothy. Again McArthur's commentary on the NKJV is helpful: "Some of the women in Ephesus probably overreacted to the cultural denigration they had typically suffered and took advantage of their opportunity in the church by seeking a dominant role in leadership. Paul forbids women from exercising any type of authority over men in the church assembly, since the elders are those who rule. They (the elders) are all to be men."

SO WHAT?

So can a woman teach the high school boys? Can a woman teach in a staff meeting with volunteer male workers present? May the woman be the youth pastor if she has men under her? May the woman be in a paid staff position of any kind? May a woman give announcements if a man is present?

You must answer these for yourself because you will give an account before the Lord. Allow me to share some of my convictions based on my understandings of the affirmations and boundaries of Scripture. My clothing must be modest as a minister so as to not distract other worshippers. As a woman, my attitude must be that of willing submission to the authority under which I serve. I must exercise self-control over my words, my thoughts, my actions, my reactions to others in all settings. I need to be an active learner spiritually. I personally choose to teach by invitation of the pastor under whom I serve.

Tonight, for instance, the senior high youth pastor at my church (age twenty-five and a former student of mine from Christian Heritage College) is on a mission trip out of the country. Even though I am more than twice his age, I gladly volunteer on his staff and follow his leadership in all things. Last week, he called me and asked if I would be willing to share my life testimony with our youth group. I was delighted to share regarding God's work in my life. I will do so tonight with male volunteers present because my attitude is right, I am under authority, and I will be dressed modestly.

I personally have presented in chapels at four different Christian colleges at the invitation of a campus pastor, the college president, or a denominational leader. I always place the podium off to the side to help soften the authority that the podium suggests. I study hard and learn all I can about the text I am presenting.

I believe it is wrong to hold the office of pastor/teacher since I, as a single woman, cannot be "the husband of one wife." I have served on church staff as the Director of Christian Education. I served under the authority of the pastor and deacons. I did not attend deacons' meetings. I sent proposals to them but then gladly implemented whatever they decided to do. Often they followed my proposal, as I had gained their respect as a trained professional with a proper attitude. In those particular ministries, I recruited married couples to assist in the ministry to provide adequate male role models for the teens to follow.

At three different colleges, I have taught hundreds of students Bible study skills. I have done so under the authority of my department chair, following extensive study myself, and with their blessing. In each of those situations, there were multiple sections of the class offered in case a male student did not want to learn from a female teacher.

REMINDERS FOR IMPLEMENTATION

So what's a woman to do? Maintain a right attitude—that of a meek and quiet spirit. Wait on God to open doors—not forcing them yourself before the time is right or before God deems you ready. Learn all you can about Scripture, people, and ministry by reading, observing, and taking classes. Serve whenever possible—taking attendance, preparing refreshment, making flyers, teaching a small group of girls, working one-on-one with students and other female volunteer staff. Stay true to biblical boundaries.

Men, your task is to open doors of opportunity so the women in your ministry can serve God with all they have to offer. Don't shortchange your ministry and its effectiveness because of insecurity on your part. Remember that woman was divinely designed to complete you and your ministry. I believe that every husband will give an account to the Lord at the judgment for how he empowered his mate. Likewise, church leaders—be they pastors, elders, or deacons—will be held responsible for the way they stewarded the women and their respective spiritual gifts that were entrusted to them in the work of the church. The work to be accomplished is huge—nearly 75 percent of American youth are reported to be unchurched.[4]

EGALITARIAN OR COMPLEMENTARIAN?

The topic of women's roles in ministry is a hotly debated one. Good and godly people disagree on the implications of the texts that are included in this chapter.

> Some faith communities allow all ministry roles to be filled by those called by God and affirmed by the church, irrespective of gender. Other churches believe males must fill the clergy and lay leadership roles in the local church and at denominational levels, while still others not only bar women from leadership roles, but limit them to ministries of hospitality, ministry to children, and other women.[5]

I personally strive in every way to hold Scripture as the authority over my life and actions, especially as it relates to the role of women in ministry, which has been my life's work.

NOTES

1. *Evangelical Dictionary of Christian Education*, ed. Michael Anthony (Grand Rapids, MI: Baker Books, 2001), s.v. "Women in Ministry."

2. Robert Saucy and Judith TenElshof, eds., *Men and Women in Ministry: A Complementary Perspective* (Chicago: Moody Press, 2001), 73–75.

3. John MacArthur, ed. *The MacArthur Study Bible: New King James Version* (Nashville: World Bibles, 1997), 1634.

4. Bo Boshers, "How Do We Reach Irreligious Students?" in *Reaching a*

Generation for Christ: A Comprehensive Guide to Youth Ministry by Richard
R. Dunn and Mark H. Senter, III (Chicago: Moody Press, 1997), 356.

    5. *Evangelical Dictionary of Christian Education*, ed. Michael Anthony
(Grand Rapids, MI: Baker Books, 2001), s.v. "Women in Ministry."

SUGGESTED READING

Archer, Gleason L. *Encyclopedia of Bible Difficulties*. Grand Rapids, MI: Zon-
    dervan, 1982.

Clouse, Bonnidell and Robert G. Clouse, eds. *Women in Ministry: Four
    Views*. Downers Grove, IL: InterVarsity Press, 1989.

Earle, Ralph. *Word Meanings in the New Testament*. Vol. 5, *Philippians –Phile-
    mon*. Grand Rapids, MI: Baker Books, 1977.

Elliot, Diane. "What are the Issues Women Face in Youth Ministry?" in
    *Reaching a Generation for Christ: A Comprehensive Guide to Youth Min-
    istry*. Richard Dunn and Mark Senter, eds. Wheaton, IL: Victor Books,
    1995.

Elliot, Diane and Ginny Olson, eds. *Breaking the Gender Barrier in Youth
    Ministry: The Emerging Role of Women in Youth Leadership*. Wheaton, IL:
    Victor Books, 1995.

Hosier, Helen Kooiman. *100 Christian Women Who Changed the 20th
    Century*. Grand Rapids, MI: Fleming H. Revell, 2000.

Hull, Gretchen Gaebelein. *Equal to Serve: Women and Men in the Church and
    Home*. Old Tappan, NJ: Fleming H. Revell, 1987.

Köstenberger, Andreas J., Thomas R. Schreiner, and H. Scott Baldwin, eds.
    Women in the Church: A Fresh Analysis of 1 Timothy 2:9–15. Grand
    Rapids, MI: Baker Books, 1995.

Piper, John and Wayne Grudem, eds. *Recovering Biblical Manhood and Wom-
    anhood: A Response to Evangelical Feminism*. Wheaton, IL: Crossway
    Books, 1991.

Saucy, Robert L. and Judith K. TenElshof, eds. *Men and Women in Ministry:
    A Complementary Perspective*. Chicago: Moody Press, 2001.

Vincent, Marvin. *Word Studies in the New Testament*. McLean, VA: MacDon-
    ald Publishing, n.d.

Wuest, Kenneth. *Wuest's Word Studies from the Greek New Testament: For the
    English Reader*. Vol. 2, *Philippians-Hebrews, The Parstoral Epistles—First
    Peter In These Last Days*. Grand Rapids, MI: Wm B. Eerdmans Publish-
    ing, 1952.

IT AIN'T NO
ONE-MAN SHOW

Phil Newberry

It was a hot, summer day in 1943 in the small southwest Arkansas town of DeQueen when Mr. Edwin McClain knocked on a door on the other side of the tracks. Edwin, the teen boys' Sunday school teacher at the First Baptist Church of DeQueen, was visiting a prospect for the church by the name of Dean. Edwin wanted to invite Dean, a strapping handsome young teenager, to join him and his class at the city park for a Saturday afternoon picnic/social. Edwin took Dean to the picnic and in doing so touched the future by touching one life. Sitting on the steps of the park gazebo, Edwin, a faithful youth leader, led Dean to faith in Jesus Christ.

Almost immediately, Dean felt the call on his life to preach the gospel. Going off to Bible College, Dean was called to his first church as pastor. Today, some fifty-eight years later, Dean is still a pastor in Northwest Arkansas.

That's a wonderful story of the faithfulness of a youth Sunday school teacher, but the story doesn't end there. You see, that teenage boy is my father. When Edwin McClain touched Dean's life, he touched mine as well. For over thirty years, I have served as a youth pastor and the story continues as my wife, Jeanne, and I have two children, Tyler and Natalie, who have both been called into ministry.

Edwin didn't just touch one life that summer day in 1943. He literally touched generations to come. I owe my spiritual heritage to a volunteer youth leader who invested his life into the lives of teenagers.

I love teenagers. There's nothing I'd rather do than work with teens. As I approach my fifties and complete twenty years of service to the church that called me to pastor their teens in 1985, I have a passion to reach students for Christ like never before. I truly love teenagers!

Yet, my ministry would never be complete if it were not for the volunteers that God has provided to serve with me all of these years. You see, they are the true youth pastors—the true shepherds. They are the ones who give of themselves and their time to love kids to Jesus. Paid youth pastors cannot do it without those who volunteer their time and energy. We are a team. We must be a team!

How can we develop an adult leadership team, and how can we disciple youth together? Allow me to share some basic insights God has shown to me in thirty years of ministry to youth.

IT'S NOT ABOUT ME

Rick Warren said it best in his powerful best seller *The Purpose Driven® Life*, "It's not about me." How true! As we look at how to develop a leadership team, we must understand this foundational principle; it's not about us! You see, there are many youth pastors who think the world revolves around them, that they are the means to the end, that they are the center of the universe and their church's youth ministry revolves around their very presence. Wrong! It's not about you! You were called to that church not to *be* the youth ministry but to *pastor* the youth ministry. You are there to equip the saints for the ministry of the body. Your role is to give visionary leadership to your flock. There's no such thing as a "Lone Ranger" youth pastor. Those who try to do it all themselves will crash and burn. That's one reason why some believe and teach that the average stay for a youth pastor in our country is less than two years. When you try to do it yourself, you fail your church, your family, and yourself. You will burn out! Plus, if we have a philosophy of "every member a minister," then you are robbing the laity of your church of exercising their callings and using their gifts. So, as we begin, repeat after me: "It's not about me, it's not about me, it's not about me."

Before we look into the "hows" of developing an adult leadership team, let's first look at the "whys."

WHY DEVELOP AN ADULT LEADERSHIP TEAM?

Smaller Is Better

As always, our model and example in life should be Jesus Christ. Look at how Christ led and you will find the size of His audience often changed. You see Him on the mountainside or out in a boat addressing the multitudes. There were times when a crowd had assembled in a home or in the temple. Yet, to see the greatest impact Christ had on individual lives, you will find it was in the times He was pouring His life into twenty, twelve, or even three people. Whether you are a full-time student pastor, a bi-vocational one, or a volunteer, you will find the crowd is often too big for you to make a significant impact on all of them. One person cannot adequately disciple thirty, ninety, or six hundred. You must bring other adults onto your team so that the ratio of adults to students is realistic and manageable.

Relationships Are Everything

In student ministry, relationships are everything. My leaders hear me say constantly, "Kids don't care what you know until they know that you care." True relationship building happens in small numbers. There is no way I can get to know hundreds of students individually and influence each one of them. I must develop a leadership team to have an effective ministry for touching young lives.

Why Develop a Team?

Why develop a leadership team? It is scriptural. It is practical. It prevents a ministry from being built on an individual personality. Often, when the superstar youth pastor leaves the church, the ministry falls apart because it was all built around one person. The greatest compliment you could ever give a youth pastor when he leaves the church is that the youth ministry never missed a beat because he had established a team approach and not an individual one.

Now let's look at the "hows" of building a leadership team.

HOW TO DEVELOP AN ADULT LEADERSHIP TEAM

Advisory Team

The first step in building a leadership team is to build a small advisory team of key laity. At our church, we call it the Student Education Committee. This is a group of parents and leaders who represent the masses. Different family types (traditional, blended, single-parent) as well as different school situations (public, private, home school) are represented. This group of twenty to twenty-five adults serves in an advisory and accountability role. We meet on a monthly basis to plan and implement the ministry to students at our church. Nothing happens in our ministry that has not first passed through their hands. Need a curriculum change? They research the market and select the one appropriate for our kids. Need to change camps? They discuss the options and help select the location. Have a conflict among leaders or kids or families? They are the ones to help bring resolution.

Why do I do this? Because I do not want the ministry built around me. Proverbs 15:22 says there is wisdom in the counsel of many. There are businessmen, homemakers, and other professionals, etc., who have a wealth of wisdom. This committee is everything to me. I could not do the work of youth ministry without them.

Purpose Driven

Rick Warren and Doug Fields did the church a favor when they challenged us to become purpose driven. As you look at building a leadership team, I want to encourage you to ask yourself the question, "Why do I do what I do?" If someone were to ask you to articulate in a sentence or paragraph why youth ministry exists, what would you say? Most people want to be a part of something that has purpose and meaning. They want to know where they are headed and how they will get there. To recruit a team of adults, you need to start with a specific purpose. You will find it is a lot easier to recruit people if they know why you do what you do and know where they are going.

Recruiting a Team

You have twelve kids who need someone to lead them (or maybe it is 120). Where do you go to find adults to join the team? The first place to go to recruit leaders is to your existing leadership team. They are your best recruiters. Put out the need and challenge them to look within their circle of influence. They already know the ministry and what's expected of a leader there. They can be an extension of you to recruit others to ministry.

The second place to look for adult leaders is within the parents of youth. Many younger youth pastors are intimidated when parents are around, and I can understand their apprehension. However, parents can become the biggest advocates for you and the ministry. Look at the Booster Club at school. Who are the ones manning the concession stand? The parents. Who is driving the soccer team to its next game? The parents. Most parents want to be involved in their teen's life. Use this to your advantage.

You will especially find parents of younger adolescents desiring to serve. Once you have hooked them, most will stay for the long haul. Do be careful, though, of the few who want to be there to smother their own child.

Other potential recruits are your senior adults. Kids love

their grandparents. Why not bring their grandparents on board your team? Some of your most effective leaders can be seniors and retirees. They are the prayer warriors. They are the ones making the phone calls, writing the letters, loving on the kids. Partner with your senior adult ministry, and you will find a resource gold mine.

I think of one of our junior high leaders by the name of Jeanne. In 1954 as a nursing student in Memphis, she became Bellevue Baptist Church's first paid youth director. Now, fifty years later, Jeanne is still teaching youth, and the girls love her!

One final place to recruit is within your student ministry. Utilize your college students as assistants and mentors. Call on some of your older juniors and seniors to lead and mentor your middle school kids.

Screening Your Recruits

Many times you will find you have some leaders that you would rather get rid of or retire them from youth ministry. In most cases, they are ineffective leaders because they were ineffectively recruited. You do your students, yourself, and the individual a disservice when you simply recruit someone to be a warm body in a classroom. You must be very cautious and direct when recruiting adult volunteers.

First, you must be cautious because of the culture in which we live. Your church should have a screening process before an adult is ever placed in front of teenagers. Many churches are now doing background checks on every adult working with minors. By doing so, you are protecting the teen and the church from any possible wrongdoing. You should have a detailed application for them to complete. Following the application, they should go through a face-to-face interview with you and/or key laity.

Second, you should be direct. Be very clear about your expectations. Have the "job description" in print. Paint the picture with the good, the bad, and the ugly so that they have a clear, realistic picture of what they will face.

Proper recruitment of leaders will give you a team that is committed to the purpose of your ministry.

Training Your Team

Once you have your team in place, you must train them in how to be effective youth leaders. Start by having new leader training sessions. I am amazed sometimes how we will take an adult who has never taught or been with students and simply throw him or her to the lions. When you start a new job, you go through training and orientation. School teachers go through a period of "practice teaching." There is a "farm" system in professional sports to prepare the players for the major leagues. It is much more important to train properly the people who will mold the faith of your youth.

Begin with a training period to introduce new leaders to the ministry. Train them in how to prepare a lesson and how to lead discussions. Give them guidance on how to win the right to be heard and how to effectively minister to students. Use some of your well-seasoned leaders or pros to mentor and train the rookies.

Training should continue throughout the year. As the culture changes, we must learn how to stay relevant without compromising the Word. Bring in "experts" in the field to train. As a suggestion, a seasoned youth pastor from a neighboring town could be asked to come in for a time of teacher training. Often, a visiting speaker can say with a fresh voice what you have been trying to communicate, and it finally clicks. Bring in an area school principal to discuss life on a high school campus. There are also specialists who travel the country leading training conferences for leaders.

Communication Is the Key

You are on a team, not an individual player. A team must communicate with one another. Monthly, or at the least quarterly, leadership meetings should be scheduled for your leaders to hear from your heart as you cast the vision for the ministry.

Our team meets monthly either at the church or in a home. We strive to be family friendly in our scheduling of the meetings. One reason it is hard for us to get volunteers to attend our meetings is that once we get them there, we have nothing to say. If a busy layman takes time out of his schedule to come to one of your meetings, it had better be worth his while. Make every minute count. Start on time and respect their time by ending on time.

Creative Training Options

Because our leaders are so busy, we offer what we call a "Book of the Month." It is my way to train and build them up as individuals without having to call a meeting. Each month I select a book, publicize it, and encourage the leader to order a copy, usually provided at cost. The books selected cover three areas. The first is ministry to youth (how to communicate, how to counsel, etc.). The second category is a tool to help them in the classroom, such as a commentary. The final type is something to help them personally in their walk with Christ. I will rotate through these each quarter. Not only does this allow the adult to read and learn at his or her own pace, but it also helps build personal libraries.

Another way to train and keep leaders culturally relevant is to inform them of Internet-based resources that will help them as youth leaders.

Ownership of Ministry

To develop an effective team, you must give the adults ownership of the ministry. Remember, you are not a hireling; you are a pastor. Release the ministry to them. Not only let them have a voice in the ministry, but also let them dream with you in planning for the future of the ministry. Some of the greatest changes we have ever made to our ministry to students are ideas that came through one of our volunteers. For instance, Melvin came to me years ago and said, "Phil, you preach to us 'Kids don't care what you know until they know that you care.' Yet about the time we get to know them, you promote them to the next grade and a different class." Melvin suggested we keep our classes together for two-year cycles. I took this idea to our Student Education Committee. We studied it, prayed over it, and then adopted it. Now our classes stay together for two years with the same leaders. We love it, and our kids do too. This one idea, coming from a volunteer, is one of the most significant changes ever made to our ministry.

Accountability

Any team needs accountability to be successful. This is especially true with volunteers. The principles found in Ecclesiastes 4:9–12 are of great value in forming a team. King Solomon advises us:

> Two are better than one, because they have a good reward for their labor. For if they fall, one will lift up his companion. But woe to him who is alone when he falls, for he has no one to help him up. Again, if two lie down together, they will keep warm; but how can one be warm alone? Though one may be overpowered by another, two can withstand him. And a threefold cord is not quickly broken.

You need to hold your leaders to a high level of accountability. You have delegated to them a small group of students to lead, teach, and mentor. It is your role as key leaders over them to hold them to their "job description" and expectations. Do they attend assigned meetings? Are they faithful in their attendance? Are they ministering to those students assigned to them? Are they teaching the approved curriculum? We utilize a system we call Grade Leaders and Grade Shepherds in our Sunday morning leadership team. Every leader has someone holding him or her accountable. We do the same thing on Wednesday nights through our Unit Leaders in the Discipleship In Action ministry.

Care and Feeding

Once you have your team in place, you will want to care for them as individuals and as a group. I write and call all leaders on their birthdays to wish them well. Twice a year, we provide banquets in their honor. One is an appreciation banquet where we provide a wonderful meal, program, and gift. The second banquet is at Christmas time. There they receive a simple gift. Everyone wants to feel loved and appreciated. This is necessary to keep the morale of the team up. Admit it. Youth ministry is pretty much a thankless "job." You need to take it upon yourself to show appreciation and give honor to whom honor is due. We also do in-home potluck dinners and fellowships to provide those times of *koinoinia*.

Beyond the Church Walls

You must communicate to your team that being a youth leader is more than teaching a lesson and more than showing up for a one-hour youth meeting. I try to avoid using the term "teacher" and call them leaders, mentors, and ministers. If an adult just wants to exercise his or her gift of teaching, and refuses to spend time with the kids, I usually suggest teaching in another area of the church. We must instill in our adults how important it is to "win the right to be heard." The old saying is true once again, "How do you spell love? T-I-M-E." Leaders must go beyond the church walls and spend time with their students. Stop by a ballgame where some of your youth are playing; see them at the places they work; have lunch with them at school; visit in their homes, etc. The leaders must penetrate their students' lives. If I am going to err, it will be because I did too much to reach a student, not too little.

QUALIFICATIONS OF A LEADER

What does it take to be an effective youth leader? Fortunately, it is not what it was when I started. Back then, the churches wanted a young, vivacious, "hip," cheerleader type who would keep the kids amused and entertained and out of the adults' hair. Today, thank the Lord, youth ministry has matured. Today an effective leader of youth can be anyone from a senior adult to a nerd to a single parent. They can come in all shapes and sizes and colors. Today's youth leaders, however, do need certain characteristics to truly make a difference in a student's life. Here is a list of some qualifications I look for in a youth leader at my church:

- **Genuine Love of Christ.** "For the love of Christ compels us" (2 Corinthians 5:14). No other motivation is sufficient to carry you through the rigors of working with youth over a long period; Christ's *agape* love just gives and gives without expecting a response.
- **Sincere Love for Kids.** "Love must be sincere" (Romans 12:9 NIV). Not everyone can tolerate adolescents! If you are uncomfortable with their music, jargon, dress, and style of life, it could be an indication you will have to grow to understand and love them. Do not fake it—they can spot a phony. Remember, seek first to understand.
- **Flexibility and the Ability to Hang Loose.** "Preach the word! Be ready in season and out of season. Convince, rebuke, exhort, with all longsuffering and teaching" (2 Timothy 4:2). Each class, each week, each one-on-one situation brings a different set of circumstances. If you can't flex, you will be totally frustrated.
- **Enthusiasm.** "And whatever you do, do it heartily, as to the Lord and not to men" (Colossians 3:23). Gloom and

negativism is contagious—so is enthusiasm! Serving God by ministering to youth is one of the highest callings in the kingdom of God. Serve Him—enthusiastically with all your heart.

- **Loyalty.** "By this all will know that you are My disciples, if you have love for one another" (John 13:35). If the youth leadership team functions in harmony and genuine love, it will spread to the youth. Let's support one another, empathize with one another, and encourage one another.
- **Dependability.** "Well done, good and faithful servant" (Matthew 25:21). The greatest ability is dependability! If you fulfill all your responsibilities to the best of your ability, you will honor the Lord and see a fruitful youth ministry.
- **Confidentiality.** "See then that you walk circumspectly, not as fools but as wise" (Ephesians 5:15). If a young person confides in us, you must not share it with other students or other leaders if it is gossip. In certain cases such as abuse or violence, you may be legally required to report what you hear. Do not promise confidentiality to a student.
- **Strength and Firmness.** "Be strong in the Lord and in the power of His might." (Ephesians 6:10). Remember you are a son or daughter of the King of Kings with all rights and privileges that go with it. Therefore, act like one, in royal humility. Most kids respond to strong, consistent leadership.

NO HIGHER CALLING

I believe there is no higher calling in the kingdom of God than to be a leader of teenagers. Think about it. We are touching tomorrow . . . today. God loves teenagers. Throughout His Word, we see how God uses the young to impact the world. Throughout history, we see how God has used the young to bring about spiritual awakenings. We are so blessed to be involved with students and to witness the powerful moving of the Spirit of God among them.

Don't go it alone. Assemble your team and lead them into battle. When Edwin McClain touched one life, he touched generations to come. It is our privilege to do the same. I stand with you and beside you as you

Touch tomorrow . . . today!

WHAT ARE YOU GOING TO BE WHEN YOU GROW UP?

Dr. David E. Adams

The question of youth ministry longevity is not a new issue confronting full-time youth professionals. The validity of ministering to youth as a full-time vocation past the age of thirty has been the source of debate in churches, universities, and seminaries for several years. But few contest that youth ministry is a "key component of the evangelistic strategy of many growing churches"[1] It appears that many believe in youth ministry, but few see it as a life-long ministry vocation. Often it is viewed as a transitional job for the young pastor in training. The ecclesial culture must nurture the profession of youth ministry and the longevity of youth staff members.

Veteran, experienced youth ministers are needed nationally and internationally to provide guidance and stability to the youth and their families. "Youth ministry has historically been an exercise in cross-cultural missions and historically placed as a high priority for evangelism and discipleship."[2] Youth ministry must be a respected profession that requires competent leadership to oversee the shepherding of youth and family ministry.

STAGES OF YOUTH MINISTERS' DEVELOPMENT

Youth ministers, along with those who train and supervise them, need to have an understanding and strategy of development for long-term service. A life of change is the typical experience that may be expected by those considering the career of youth and family minister. "Life transitions are normal and inevitable parts of adult life; they clarify life issues and life direction."[3] There are six basic stages of a youth minister's development:[4]

I Formation Stage (The Novice),
II Passion Stage (The Rookie),
III Maturing Stage (The Professional),
IV Family Stage (The Parent),
V Endurance Stage (The Coordinator),
VI Legacy Stage (The Elder).

These stages serve as predictors for the developing youth leader.

Stage I—Formation Stage (The Novice: 11–18 years of age)

Characteristically, this stage begins in early adolescence and usually ends by late adolescence. Many influences affect the emerging youth minister before he or she has the first interview with a search committee in consideration of a position. Piaget's "disequilibration" affirms that processes assisting people in growth and development are most prevalent during the formation stage.[5] Internal incongruence gives way to identity formation and individuality. "Growth in self-image produces growth in the teen's personality and behavior."[6]

Significant spiritual changes generally take place during the formation stage, beginning with the person becoming a Christian and incorporating the dynamic of the Spirit-filled life. He becomes aware of the significance of local church involvement and Christian service. The discipline and fulfillment of studying Scripture becomes integrative. An awareness of and a passion for the lost souls of humanity become a life focus. Consecration to the Lordship of Christ in everyday living and decision-making emerges as a practical aspect of his journey. "Self-authorization emerges with the possibility of making choices based solely on the self, apart from the dictates and expectations of the group."[7]

At this stage, the maturing Christian has an awareness of one's destiny and a sense of a divine call to youth ministry. Other significant adults, peers, parents, and ministers usually affirm this call. During the formation stage, thoughts of academic and experiential learning emerge and short- and long-range planning are articulated.

The womb of the church youth group incubates the developing ministerial student. Imprinting occurs as the young person identifies and assumes the role of a future minister. He is growing in the mental competencies necessary for leadership. "Mental operations are no longer limited to concrete objects; they can be applied to purely verbal or logical statements, to the possible as well as the real, to the future as well as the present."[8] Sermonic rhetoric is more easily interpreted, assimilated, and implemented.

Stage II—Passion Stage (The Rookie: 19–25 years of age)

Upon graduation from high school, the emerging youth minister identifies an institution of higher learning where she may be formally trained for youth ministry. The selection of a compatible learning site is a vital decision. The wrong choice can be detrimental to her growth, vision, passion, and strategy. She should choose based on her vision for future ministry. It is during this stage that she matriculates through not less than five levels of training: student, apprenticeship, intern, resident, and professional.[9]

As a *student*, essential cognitive competencies are identified and learned. General studies, Bible knowledge, and social sciences are mastered, culminating in a bachelor's degree and, possibly, graduate studies. Serving as an *apprentice*, the student discovers the church to be an observatory for experiential learning. As an *intern*, the student begins his field education under the tutelage of a veteran youth minister. The passionate trainee progresses to the *resident* level, having qualified for church employment and leadership. Finally, the *professional* youth minister is placed in his first church as *the* youth and family minister.

A potential danger is a singularity of focus that may dominate the rookie youth minister to a level of obsession. He has something to prove to himself and to all who have invested in him. As a driven person, he has "an increasing inability to separate role from person. What he does is indistinguishable from who he is."[10] In this phase, he experiences a vocational adrenalin rush that displays itself as workaholism. No phone call is too late, no distance is too far, and no personal sacrifice is too demanding when it comes to ministering to his students. A ministerial narcissism emerges in his universe. Everything is precious: the desk, the phone, the office, the calendar, and each student. He has the best pastor, the best facilities, and the greatest job God ever gave to a human. Tasks are performed with enthusiasm and specificity. The rookie is appreciative of everything and everyone, even those who are not supportive. He serves with a joyous self-absorption of a ministerial honeymoon passion, romance, and first love. Relationships with students are something to enjoy, not evaluate. In his early- to mid-twenties, he is close enough to the early and middle adolescent that relating to them is natural; he is one of them, just a little older.

The rookie has a mystic vision enveloped in idealism. Frequently he has energy bursts that drive him to get things started. He easily can become overextended but thrives on superficial martyrdom to do ministry. Ministry honeymoons are normal, but they are temporary and cannot be sustained long-term. Often a church will expect their youth minister to sustain this phase indefinitely, resulting in unrealistic expectations, guilt, and the imposition of false guilt to return to the first love.

Frequently, youth ministers get married during this stage. Their marriage partner, experiencing the same phase, joins the rookie on the quest. Ministry and marriage become entwined into a single unit, energized by a blend of late adolescent normality and first church euphoria, reinforced by role stereotyping. As the youth minister nears the end of this stage, internal and external disharmony often occur.

Stage III—Maturing Stage (The Professional: 26–32 years of age)

This stage emerges with the reality that the ministerial honeymoon is over. Youth ministry is work—requiring you to pace yourself. In retrospect, the youth minister entering this stage recognizes the ministry call but now views it volitionally, a career choice. "Occupational choice is a developmental process; it is not a single decision, but a series of decisions made over a period of years."[11] No longer fueled by youthful zeal, the youth pastor seriously assesses, adjusts, plans, and executes his role. The childish novelty of the passion stage is behind, and a mature adult assumes his responsibility and privilege of service. Overnight activities, long van rides, and typical youth functions are no longer that much fun personally. Such events facilitate ministry but are not something he would do on his day off.

She is not "one of the teens" because of proximity of age. The professional stage assumes the role as an associate pastor, a leader of adolescents, a minister to families. This involves a new level of effort and work. She is adjusting to getting older and manifesting the characteristics of a "called person"[12] who:

1. Knows exactly who she is,
2. Possesses an unwavering sense of purpose,
3. Understands unswerving commitment, and
4. Has a peacefulness about her, which is not tied to the security of a career.

There is a loss of ministry innocence at the outset of this stage. Gone is the heightened concern to please pastor, parents, and students. The validity of conformity is objectively assessed. "We make a lot of effort to conform to other people's expectations, sometimes to our benefit and other times to our detriment."[13] The maturing youth minister assumes the reigns of his life by taking the initiative for personal growth, launching a life-long learning strategy as an adult learner.

He possesses three qualifying characteristics for the position: "theological consistency, rapport with youth, and team leadership."[14] He becomes a valued member of the church staff, assuming the role of resident youth and family expert. As an expository preacher/teacher, he also possesses comprehensive and functional knowledge of youth culture, adolescent characteristics, trends, group dynamics, and counseling skill. A serious review of things learned in school, an introspective assessment of personal competencies, a ministry audit, and the implementation of long-term strategy are characteristic of this stage.

Idealism and realism are embraced as partners of successful ministry. As such, the youth leader becomes politically astute. Successful ministry requires tenure. Tenure demands skills in the internal systems of the church. Annual reviews, policy manuals, personnel committees, budget procedures, and a multiplicity of protocols, are not avoided but are viewed as contributors to effectiveness. The youth minister becomes a respected peer among the staff.

Stage IV—Family Stage (The Parent: 32–45 years of age)

As years have passed, the developing youth minister has become established as a professional. No longer a late adolescent or a young adult, he has developed as a family man with personal and professional time-management pressures. With the birth of each child "another level of maturity is achieved."[15] Operating from a divine sense of calling, he becomes acutely sensitive to home. "The leader cannot spend time on secondary matters while essential obligations scream for attention."[16] Authentic Christianity is now of paramount importance, and his family becomes the reflection of true self. Each child is a reminder of the minister's leadership role and responsibility.

Simultaneously the youth leader is confronted with responsibilities to the church and its leadership. Calendar planning, a joyful experience as a rookie, is now a stressful task. Children's education, social events, and spiritual development are pressing duties. Fulfilling her spouse through quality and quantity of time are an exciting challenge. Time is life and life requires allotment of time.

It is during this stage that the youth leader may experience a role identity crisis. Today's youth pastor must maneuver through a complexity of roles: expectations of the spouse, senior pastor, church leaders, youth lay staff, and children's authorities. It is during this stage that these challenges are addressed, adding to the credentials and appeal of the youth minister.

As the mission of the church is implemented, the youth leader is experiencing her most productive years to date. She is learning to prioritize family and church into a holistic lifestyle.

Stage V—Endurance Stage (The Coordinator: 46–60 years of age)

The largest youth organization in westernized countries is the public school system. In this system, those who train students are developmentally affirmed as professionals. The teacher expects to retire from the educational profession. The organization assists the transitioning professional through his stages of life and career path. Though not fully realized today, in like fashion the church is beginning to feel the professional effect of the school system's influence. It is shaping the environment for today's youth professional. Youth pastors are older, academically and experientially credentialed, staying in their churches longer, earning salaries commensurate with schoolteachers,[17] and achieving professional status. Churches are no longer hiring only the "novice" and the "rookie" youth ministers. During the endurance stage, there is a multiplicity of internal and external developments.

The coordinator has earned the status of a leader of adults plus the respect of parents. He now has a significant influence on the church staff. While doing hands-on work with a small group of adolescents and coordinating the high school ministry, his focus is the investment of substantial time and resources into his lay and paid staff. He has raised his own children and authoritatively ministers to parents and grandparents. His developmental path has moved him into the second half of his life. During his journey, he has turned down opportunities for other ministerial roles. Introspection, career assessment, and spiritual renegotiation have brought him to this stage. He is self-actualized spiritually, and he functionally realizes Christ satisfies his needs.

During this stage, he has accepted life's station, and passion is redefined beyond the "novice" emotion. Staff and committees become his partners in determining personal operations and budget. He was once viewed as a son/child minister who should be grateful to have a job. Now he is perceived as a seasoned veteran leading the youth and family ministry.

During this stage, there is retooling initiated by self-development, self-motivation, and a sense of destiny. There are three categories of environmental factors that affect his job satisfaction: "preferred supervision, preferred teamwork, and preferred conditions."[18] More than ever, he is operating out of a sense of calling, armed with a strategic plan to advance the kingdom.

The coordinator perceives himself as a part of the ministry whole. His joy is the participation in a divine movement that may be defined as "the collective activity of committed, multiplying disciples as they band together and trust God for an impact greater than their own individual ministries."[19] As a parental "empty nester," he and his spouse are able to focus on the strategic plan together. At the top of his game professionally, he approaches ministry with revitalization.

Stage VI—Legacy Stage (The Elder: 60 and beyond)

The paramount crisis of this stage is confronting one's mortality. In addition to confronting death, no less than five crises are addressed: "loss of finances, loss of self-esteem, loss of work-oriented social contacts, loss of meaningful tasks, and loss of a reference group."[20] With retirement looming, individuals at this stage come to personal resolution for life impact. Life meaning is fueled by life purpose.

He becomes "someone who not only is competent at doing something but is competent at being human as well—a mensch, a complete person."[21] During this stage, the youth minister crystallizes "the importance of developing people to share in and assist you with the implementation of his dreams as a leader. The thesis is: *The more people you develop, the greater the extent of your dreams.*"[22]

It is in this context that he has nothing to prove to anyone, only a destiny to fulfill, a life to be appreciatively lived, a legacy to deposit. The role of grandparent permeates the youth minister during this stage. "The reward they want is that they have contributed, personally, to something greater than themselves."[23] It is through biological and spiritual offspring that such a reward is obtained. The question must be asked, "What type of mentor/grandparent will the youth leader become?"

Circumstances, individual uniqueness, and Holy Spirit leading determine this. He desires to leave his imprint on future generations. He draws upon his life's accomplishments, connections, resources, and creative energy to implement the dream that lasts beyond his lifetime, "living and serving under the burden of the original vision."[24] He uses his position and influence to perpetuate his legacy.

* * *

Today's youth and family minister is a developing individual who is part of the emerging profession. Developmental theories are absolute truth. "The life cycle is like a kaleidoscope turning—while there are predictable features to the changing patterns, there are also random and never-ending surprises."[25] The stages of ministry life for the youth minister are a guide to suggest the normality of life transitions. An understanding of the stages of ministry for the youth minister should add to the preparedness for youth workers desiring to have longevity of ministry.

NOTES

1. Thom Rainer, *Effective Evangelistic Churches* (Nashville, TN: Broadman and Holman, 1996), 96.

2. James H. Scroggins IV, "A Proposal for the Training of Indigenous Youth Workers for The International Mission Board of the Southern Baptist Convention" (PhD diss., Southern Baptist Theological Seminary, 2003), 2.

3. Frederic M. Hudson, *The Adult Years: Mastering the Art of Self-renewal* (San Francisco, CA: Jossey-Bass Publishing, 1999), 100.

4. David E. Adams and Douglas Randlett, "Stages of Youth Ministry" (lecture, Liberty University, Lynchburg, VA, September 17, 1993).

5. Roger W. Bybee and Robert B. Sund, *Piaget for Educators* (Prospect Heights, IL: Waveland Press, 1990), 190.

6. Elmer L. Towns, *Successful Biblical Youth Work* (Nashville, TN: Impact Books, 1973), 123.

7. James C. Wilhoit and John M. Dettoni, *Nurture That Is Christian* (Grand Rapids, MI. BridgePoint Books, 1995), 80.

8. Patricia H. Miller, *Theories of Developmental Psychology* (New York: W. H. Freeman, 1993), 42.

9. David E. Adams, "The Development of Youth Ministry as a Professional Career and the Distinctives of Liberty University Youth Ministry Training in Preparing Students for Youth Work" (DM thesis, Liberty University, 1993), 144.

10. Gordon McDonald, *Ordering Your Private World* (Nashville, TN: Thomas Nelson, 1985), 54.

11. Herr 1979, 91. Boston, MA: Little, Brown, and Company, 1979) p. 91

12. Gordon McDonald, *Ordering Your Private World* (Nashville, TN: Thomas Nelson,1985), 54.

13. Ralph Mattson and Thom Black, *Discovering Your Child's Design* (Elgin, IL: David C. Cook, 1989), 46.

14. Paul Borthwick, *How to Choose a Youth Pastor* (Nashville, TN: Thomas Nelson, 1993), 92.

15. Gordon Luff, interview by the author, February 17, 2006

16. J. Oswald Sanders, *Spiritual Leadership* (Chicago: Moody Press, 1994), 94.

17. *Group* Magazine, vol. 32, no. 1, November/December 2005, 72.

18. David J. Frahm, *The Great Niche Hunt* (Colorado Springs, CO: NavPress, 1991), 96.

19. Bill Bright, *How to Make Your Mark* (Colorado Springs, CO: Campus Crusade for Christ, 1983), 52.

20. Marcia Lasswell and Thomas E. Lasswell, *Marriage and Family* (Lexington, MA: Heath Publishing, 1982), 459.

21. Daniel J. Levinson, *The Seasons of a Man's Life* (New York: Knopf Publishing, 1978), 97.

22. John C. Maxwell, *Developing the Leader within You* (Nashville, TN: Thomas Nelson, 1993), 113.

23. Frederic M. Hudson, *The Adult Years: Mastering the Art of Self-renewal* (San Francisco, CA: Jossey-Bass Publishing, 1999), 180.

24. Jerry Falwell, *Falwell: An Autobiography.* (Lynchburg, VA: Liberty House Publishers, 1997), 481.

25. Frederic M. Hudson, *The Adult Years: Mastering the Art of Self-renewal* (San Francisco, CA: Jossey-Bass Publishing, 1999), 129.

REFERENCES

Adams, David E. 1993. *The Development of Youth Ministry as a Professional Career and the Distinctives of Liberty University Youth Ministry Training in Preparing Students for Youth Work.* Doctor of Ministry thesis, Liberty University.

Adams, David E. and Douglas Randlett. 1991. "Stages of Youth Ministry." A classroom presentation at Liberty University for YM 403.

Borthwick, Paul. 1993. *How to Choose a Youth Pastor.* Nashville, TN: Thomas Nelson Publishing.

Bright, Bill. 1983. *How to Make Your Mark.* Colorado Springs, CO: Campus Crusade for Christ.

Buford, Bob. 1994. *Half Time.* Grand Rapids, MI: Zondervan Publishing House.

Bugelski, B. R. 1971. *The Psychology of Learning Applied to Teaching.* Indianapolis, IN: Bobbs-Merrill Company.

Bybee, Roger W. and Robert B. Sund. 1990. *Piaget for Educators.* Prospect Heights, IL: Waveland Press.

Cramer, Stanley H. and Edwin L. Herr. 1979. *Career Guidance through the Life Span.* Boston: Little, Brown and Company.

Egan, Kieran. 2002. *Getting It Wrong from the Beginning.* Grand Rapids, MI: Vail-Ballou Publishers.

Estep Jr., James Riley. 2003. *C. E. The Heritage of Christian Education.* Joplin, MO: College Press.

Falwell, Jerry. 1997. *Falwell an Autobiography.* Lynchburg, VA: Liberty House.

Fowler, J. 1981. *Stages of Faith: The Psychology of Human Development and the Quest for Meaning.* San Francisco, CA: Harper & Row.

Frahm, David J. 1991. *The Great Niche Hunt.* Colorado Springs, CO: Nav-Press.

Grunlan, Stephen A. 1984. *Marriage and Family.* Grand Rapids, MI: Academie Books.

Hall, G. Stanley. 1924. *Adolescence Volume II.* New York: D. Appelton and Company.

Harsh, Charles M. 1959. *Personality Development and Assessment.* New York, NY: The Ronald Press Company.

Hendricks, Howard G. 1973. *Heaven Help the Home.* Wheaton, IL: Victor Books.

Hudson, Frederic M. 1999. *The Adult Years: Mastering the Art of Self-renewal.* San Francisco, CA: Jossey-Bass Publishing.

Lasswell, Marcia, and Thomas E. Lasswell. 1982. *Marriage and Family.* Lexington, MA: Heath Publishing.

Levinson, Daniel J. 1978. *The Seasons of a Man's Life.* New York: Knopf Publishing.

Loder, James E. 1998. *The Logic of the Spirit.* San Francisco: Josssey-Bass Publishing.

Luff, Gordon. 1979. A personal interview conducted by the writer in Lynchburg, VA.

McDonald, Gordon. 1985. *Ordering Your Private World.* Nashville, TN: Thomas Nelson.

Mattson, Ralph and Thom Black. 1989. *Discovering Your Child's Design.* Elgin, IL: David C. Cook.

Maxwell, John C. 1993. *Developing the Leader within You.* Nashville, TN: Thomas Nelson.

Miller, Patricia H. 1993. *Theories of Developmental Psychology.* New York: W. H. Freeman.

Rainer, Thom. 1996. *Effective Evangelistic Churches*. Nashville, TN: Broadman and Holman.

Sanders, J. Oswald. 1994. *Spiritual Leadership*. Chicago: Moody Press.

Scroggins IV, James H. 2003. "A Proposal for the Training of Indigenous Youth Workers for The Internatinal Mission Board of the Southern Baptist Convention." Ph.D. diss., Southern Baptist Theological Seminary.

Senter III, Mark. 1992. *The Coming Revolution in Youth Ministry*. Wheaton, IL: Victor Books.

Super, D.E. 1953. A theory of vocational development. *American Psychologist*, 1953, 185–190.

Towns, Elmer L. 1973. *Successful Biblical Youth Work*. Nashville, TN: Impact Books.

Wilhoit, James C. and John M. Dettoni. 1995. *Nurture That is Christian*. Grand Rapids, MI: BridgePoint Books.

CONTRIBUTING WRITERS

Dr. Dave Adams—With thirty-six years of experience in student ministry, Dr. Adams serves as the Executive Director of the International Center for Youth Ministry at Boyce College and Southern Seminary, Louisville, Kentucky, since 1999.

Tim Ahlgrim—National Director for Vision For Youth, a national network of youth workers that seeks to train and encourage youth workers and students for ministry. He has worked with students for the last 32 years—23 as a youth pastor. Along with his work with Vision For Youth, he teaches youth ministry at the Crossroads Bible College in Indianapolis. He is also a wrestling coach at Lafayette Jefferson High School and serves as the Huddle Coach for the Jeff Fellowship of Christian Athletes.

Glenn Amos—His thirty-two years of experience in student ministry has included youth pastoring, educating, and pasturing. Amos now serves as Vice President of Enrollment Management at Baptist Bible College in Clarks Summit, Pennsylvania.

Ben Brown—Now serving as Associate Pastor of Adult Ministries at Pleasant View Bible Church, Warsaw, Indiana, Brown has ten years of experience in student ministry.

Mike Calhoun—Currently the Vice President of Local Church Ministries for Word of Life Fellowship, Inc., in Schroon Lake, New York, Calhoun has thirty-three years of experience in student ministry.

Calvin Carr—This Youth Pastor at First Baptist Church, Jacksonville, Florida, has twenty-five years of experience in student ministry.

Dr. Cheryl Fawcett—With thirty-two years of experience in student ministry, this former professor at Cedarville University and Christian Heritage College is now serving as international student ministry educator for Vision For Youth International and Association of Baptists for World Evangelism in El Cajon, California.

Ric Garland—Now serving as Vice President of Bible Institute Ministries for Word of Life Fellowship, Inc., in Schroon Lake, New York, Garland has twenty-seven years of experience in student ministry.

Eric Hystad—With twenty-six years of experience in student ministry, Hystad is New Campus Pastor at Second Baptist Church in Houston, Texas.

Alex McFarland—After eighteen years of experience in student ministry, McFarland is now serving as Director of Teen Apologetics for Focus on the Family in Colorado Springs, Colorado, and as President of Southern Evangelical Seminary at Veritas Graduate School of Religion in Charlotte, North Carolina.

Phil Newberry—During his more than thirty years of experience in student ministry, Newberry formerly served at First Baptist Church in Dallas, Texas. Since 1985, he is serving as Minister of Students at Bellevue Baptist Church in Memphis, Tennessee.

Dwight Peterson—Now teaching at Baptist Bible College in Clarks Summit, Pennsylvania, Peterson has twenty-five years of experience in student ministry.

Tom Phillips—With thirty-three years of experience in student ministry, Phillips is now serving as the Vice President of Florida Camping and Bible Institute Ministries for Word of Life Fellowship, Inc., in Schroon Lake, New York.

Dr. Steve Vandegriff—Now serving as the Executive Director of the Center for Youth Ministry at Liberty University in Lynchburg, Virginia, Dr. Vandegriff has over 25 years of experience in student ministry.

Dr. Lee Vukich—The Executive Director of the Center for Youth Ministry at Liberty University in Lynchburg, Virginia, Vukich has seventeen years of experience in student ministry.

Mel Walker—With thirty years of experience in student ministry as a youth pastor, educator, writer, and conference speaker, Walker is now serving as Director of Student Ministries for Regular Baptist Press and as President of Vision For Youth, which he founded.